Pandemonium!
(a Greek Myth-adventure)

Jenifer Toksvig

A Samuel French Acting Edition

SAMUELFRENCH-LONDON.CO.UK
SAMUELFRENCH.COM

Copyright © 2002 by Jenifer Toksvig (book and lyrics)
All Rights Reserved

PANDEMONIUM! is fully protected under the copyright laws of the British Commonwealth, including Canada, the United States of America, and all other countries of the Copyright Union. All rights, including professional and amateur stage productions, recitation, lecturing, public reading, motion picture, radio broadcasting, television and the rights of translation into foreign languages are strictly reserved.

ISBN 978-0-573-08117-0

www.samuelfrench-london.co.uk

www.samuelfrench.com

FOR AMATEUR PRODUCTION ENQUIRIES

UNITED KINGDOM AND WORLD EXCLUDING NORTH AMERICA

plays@SamuelFrench-London.co.uk

020 7255 4302/01

Each title is subject to availability from Samuel French,
depending upon country of performance.

CAUTION: Professional and amateur producers are hereby warned that *PANDEMONIUM!* is subject to a licensing fee. Publication of this play does not imply availability for performance. Both amateurs and professionals considering a production are strongly advised to apply to the appropriate agent before starting rehearsals, advertising, or booking a theatre. A licensing fee must be paid whether the title is presented for charity or gain and whether or not admission is charged.

The professional rights in this play are controlled by Samuel French Ltd, 52 Fitzroy Street, London, W1T 5JR.

No one shall make any changes in this title for the purpose of production. No part of this book may be reproduced, stored in a retrieval system, or transmitted in any form, by any means, now known or yet to be invented, including mechanical, electronic, photocopying, recording, videotaping, or otherwise, without the prior written permission of the publisher. No one shall upload this title, or part of this title, to any social media websites.

The right of Jenifer Toksvig to be identified as author of this work has been asserted by her in accordance with Section 77 of the Copyright, Designs and Patents Act 1988

PANDEMONIUM! (A GREEK MYTH-ADVENTURE)

Guildford

First staged at the Yvonne Arnaud Theatre, Guildford, on 28th June 2001 by the Yvonne Arnaud Youth Theatre ACT 2 with the following cast:

Pandora	Adele Sinclair	α Alpha	Emma Lumb
Epimetheus	Ben Avis	β Beta	Natasha Ho
Zeus	Philip Hammond	δ Delta	Stephanie Napier
Hera	Lucy Willis	ε Epsilon	Sarah Slater
Eros	Kristian Baker	ζ Zeta	India McLennan
Daedalus	Philip Bishop	η Eta	Jo Wright
Icarus	Ben Watley	θ Theta	Marie Kenyon
Narcissus	Robert Slater	ι Iota	Jo Brady
Echo	Lucy Hill	κ Kappa	Erin Williamson
Midas	Ollie Dawe	λ Lambda	Mary Sanderson
Dionysus	Sarah Dodson	μ Mu	Jane Sanderson
Orpheus	Matt Veira	ν Nu	Helen Pettengell
Eurydice	Natalie Bolding	ξ Xi	Louise Hewitt
Hades & Charon	Edward Kelland	π Pi	Lizzie Bourne
Theseus	Harry Burgess	ς Sigma	Jenny May
Perseus	Adrian Thompson	τ Tau	Holly Rubenstein
Heracles	Tim Slater	χ Chi	Vicky Lazzari
Odysseus	William Slater	ω Omega	Jane Avis

Directed by **Julia Burgess**
Assistant Director **Jenifer Toksvig**
Musical Director **David Perkins**
Lighting Design by **John Harris**
Sound Design by **Dan Last**

The Show in Development

New York

Originally performed in a reading at The Black Box Theatre, New York, on 10th April 2001 with the following cast:

Echo, Eurydice, Theseus	Farah Alvin
Hera, Charon	Wanda L. Houston
Icarus, Midas, Jason, Demon	Rob Maitner
Zeus, Cab Driver	Raymond Jaramillo McLeod
Orpheus, Daedalus, Dionysus, Odysseus	Kevyn Morrow
Epimetheus, Heracles	Jeffrey Todd
Hades, Eros, Narcissus, Perseus	Michael Winther
Pandora	Kristin Woodbury

Directed by **Sturgis Warner**
Musical Director **Mat Eisenstein**

Edinburgh

Further developed at the Edinburgh Festival, August 2001, with the following cast:

Pandora (Keyboards, Percussion, Tenor Sax)	Kate Buxton
Hermes, Icarus, Midas, Odysseus, Perseus, Theseus (Percussion)	Neil Clench
Dionysus, Zeus (Clarinet, Guitar, Keyboards, Percussion)	Richard Costello
Hera, Narcissus, Voice of the Box (Bassoon, Keyboards, Percussion)	Matthew Frankland-Coombes
Echo, Eros (Flute, Percussion)	Emma Manton
Daedalus, Epimetheus, Hades (Alto Sax, Bassoon)	Toby Mitchell

Directed by **Ellie Jones**
Musical Director **Matthew Frankland-Coombes**
Lighting Design by **John Harris**
Sound Design by **Chris Eley**

CONTENTS

	Page
Important Information	vi
Author's Notes	
Character Breakdown	vii
Song Notes	xii
Composer's Notes	xvi
Set and Properties, Constume, Lighting and Sound Effects	xix
Staging	xx
Synopsis of Musical Numbers	xxii
Synopsis of Scenes	xxv
Acknowledgements	xxvi
Dedication	xxvii
Other titles by Jenifer Toksvig and David Perkins	xxviii
PANDEMONIUM (a Greek Myth-adventure)	1
Furniture and Property List	62
Lighting Plot	66
Effects Plot	71
The Original Greek Myths	73

IMPORTANT INFORMATION

Alterations to the script or score
If changes, additions or cuts to the show are required to make it work for a particular group, any proposed alterations (no matter how small) MUST be approved by the authors before rehearsals commence. Approval can be sought via Samuel French Ltd (Musical Plays Department) or directly from the authors via email. An email link for Jenifer Toksvig and David Perkins can be found at their website: www.toksvigperkins.com.

The authors are happy to provide suggestions for such things as song cuts, scene change music, additional character names, and so on. Making contact with them is easy, and they will consider any request. Making small changes this way is free of charge, and it turns an illegal alteration into a legal one.

Cover illustration
Please note that the cover illustration remains the copyright of the artist, Simon Pearsall, and the author, Jenifer Toksvig. Permission MUST be obtained prior to use of this illustration for publicity purposes, programmes, website graphics, or any other purpose whatsoever. Please contact Samuel French Ltd for full details. More information about Simon Pearsall can be found via the authors' website: www.toksvigperkins.com.

Costume hire
Costumes from the original production at the Yvonne Arnaud Theatre, Millbrook, Guildford, Surrey, GU1 3UX, may be available for hire. Please contact the theatre direct.

Video and audio recording
In certain circumstances, permission may be given for a video or audio recording of your show to be made. Please apply to Samuel French Ltd for full details. Video and audio recordings made without prior permission are STRICTLY not allowed, even for archival or training purposes.

Toksvig-Perkins musicals
The authors' website at www.toksvigperkins.com has photographs of the original production, sound bites, and other useful information (including details of other shows written by Toksvig-Perkins). Jenifer and David welcome your comments in their message board and guestbook, as well as emailed photographs of your production.

AUTHOR'S NOTES

Character Breakdown

The show can be adapted to suit the number of people desired in the cast. The Greek Chorus can be played by one group or split into different groups, thus allowing more people to take part. (See **Greek Chorus**.) However, one group is preferable. (It is also possible for the Greek Chorus to be played by the Principals. Please contact the authors for more information.)

In this show, some characters are immortal (all the 'gods') and some mortal (everyone else). Prior to Pandora opening the Box and releasing Evil into the world, there is no Evil there at all. Therefore all the mortal characters are described the way they are before they're afflicted with Evils from the Box. Their specific Evil afflictions are also listed, which obviously affect their characters accordingly after the Box is opened. Immortal characters, who do not live on Earth, have always had Evil characteristics, so their character descriptions include both "good" and "bad" traits.

Different regional accents can be used for the main characters if required. This can be particularly useful if some actors are playing more than one main part, which is possible in this show. (Please contact the authors for more information.)

MAIN PARTS

Zeus (King of the Gods)
Zeus is handsome, forty-ish, well-spoken, boyishly charming, flirtatious, petulant, slightly naïve and a little bit clumsy when it comes to common sense. He's very unhappy about the lack of respect he's getting from the mortals on Earth, and he's bored with ruling over good. A bratty, villainesque ruler of the universe!
SONGS: Swing!; Pandemonium! (solo); You're The Only One Who's King (duet); The "It-Takes-Two-To-Tango" Tango (duet); Keep The Faith

Hera (Queen of the Gods)
Appearing to be in a very well-kept early-forties, Hera is elegant, attractive, proud, jealous, flirtatious, and has a tendency to be addicted when something

takes her fancy. She's highly-strung, and constantly suspicious of Zeus because of his history of philandering. This character is female, but works well as a man in drag and can be cast thus if required.
SONGS: Swing!; Pandemonium!; Stop! (solo); Keep The Faith

Eros (God of Love)
Eros is enthusiastic, determined and kind. A cheeky chappie, he spends his time trying to smooth over the path of love. This character is traditionally male, but works very well as a female if required.
SONGS: Swing!; Pandemonium!; You're The Only One Who's King! (duet); Keep The Faith

Epimetheus (A God, Creator of the Animals)
A young man, with average looks, Epimetheus is creative, a dreamer, and very intelligent. He's sweet, shy, not very good with women, and about to get married to a woman he's never even met. She runs away on their wedding day. Things are not good.
SONGS: Swing!; Pandemonium!; Wildest Dreams (solo); Wildest Dreams—Reprise No. 1 (solo); Wildest Dreams—Reprise No. 2 (duet); Some Day; Keep The Faith

Pandora (Epimetheus' mortal bride)
Made out of clay by Zeus, Pandora is brand new and, curiously, more than a little naïve. Her journey is one of discovery. She is innocent, smart, attractive, in her early twenties, and surprisingly grounded. She can even be slightly petulant. (She does take after her father, after all.)
EVIL: She comes from Zeus with Curiosity already installed.
SONGS: Swing!; Pandemonium!; Moving On (solo); Wildest Dreams (small duet); Wildest Dreams—Reprise No. 2 (duet); Some Day; Keep The Faith

Hades (God of the Underworld)
He's sharp-suited, silver-tongued, and the consummate professional. He rules over Evil with devotion and efficiency, and he dances a mean Tango, too. Mature, elegant, sophisticated and rotten to the core. This character is traditionally male, but also works very well as a female role (with a low, bluesy vocal range).
SONGS: Swing!; The "It-Takes-Two-To-Tango" Tango (duet); Keep The Faith

Daedalus (Famous mortal architect and inventor)
Daedalus is a simple man with a passion for experimenting. He's elderly, creative and very down-to-earth. When he's creating, he's keen, optimistic,

and loves problem-solving. Essentially, he's a bricks-and-mortar builder at heart.
EVIL: Pride
SONGS: Swing!; Pandemonium!; Look At Young Icarus Fly (duet); Some Day (solo line); Keep The Faith

Icarus (Daedalus' son)
A simple teenager, in awe of his father. This character can be played by a girl portraying a young boy if required.
EVIL: Adolescence!
SONGS: Swing!; Pandemonium!; Look At Young Icarus Fly (duet); Some Day (solo line); Keep The Faith

Orpheus (The greatest musician on Earth)
He's a slightly grungy, hippie rock star who adores his wife more than anything else in the world. His musical talents are phenomenal, and he spends his life hanging out with the Cool Crowd. He's kind-hearted, confident and very friendly.
EVIL: Doubt
SONGS: Swing!; Pandemonium!; Look At Young Icarus Fly (solo line); How? (solo). Some Day (solo line); Keep The Faith

Eurydice (Orpheus' wife)
She's a hippie rock chick who adores her husband more than anything else in the world. Eurydice is sweet, caring and in tune with the universe.
EVIL: Pestilence
SONGS: Swing!; Pandemonium!; Look At Young Icarus Fly (solo line); Some Day (solo line); Keep The Faith

King Midas (Ruler of Phrygia)
Midas is middle-aged, well-fed, and ridiculously rich ... but he's very generous with his money, and makes huge contributions to charity. He's gregarious, and is often the life and soul of a party. Dionysus has been his best friend for a long time.
EVIL: Greed
SONGS: Swing!; Pandemonium!; Look At Young Icarus Fly (solo line); Gold Fever (solo); Some Day (solo line); Keep The Faith

Dionysus (God of Wine and Revelry)
Dionysus has a mischievous sense of humour. He's middle-aged, a jolly drunk who likes to play innocent practical jokes. He loves spending time with his good friend, Midas.
SONGS: Swing!; Pandemonium!; Some Day (solo line); Keep The Faith

Narcissus (The most beautiful mortal on Earth)
This young man is absolutely gorgeous. He's in his early twenties, and is completely self-effacing. He adores Echo, and sees her as beautiful because he loves her for the person she is inside.
EVIL: Vanity
SONGS: Swing!; Pandemonium!; Look At Young Icarus Fly (solo line); Say That You Love Me (duet); Some Day (solo line); Keep The Faith

Echo (Narcissus' girlfriend, a Nymph of the Woods)
This young lady is in her early twenties. She's very plain, and bespectacled due to being optically short-sighted. She's terribly well-behaved, morally sound, highly intelligent, studious, and rather serious most of the time. Echo's heart catches fire when Narcissus takes her hand. She adores him.
EVIL: Gossipry
SONGS: Swing!; Pandemonium!; Look At Young Icarus Fly (solo line); Say That You Love Me (duet), Some Day (solo line); Keep The Faith

Theseus, Perseus, Odysseus (Brave and daring heroes of Earth)
These young men are good-looking, fit, eager and not terribly bright. They're everything you could want in a mythical hero, minus the brain cells.
EVIL: Arrogance
SONGS: Swing!; Pandemonium!; Look At Young Icarus Fly (solo lines); Stop! (backing vocals); Lullaby (trio); Keep The Faith

Hermes (Messenger of Olympus)
He's the delivery service of Olympus, keen and swift of foot. This character makes a brief appearance only, and can be played as a female if required.
SONGS: (As per Greek Chorus)

Charon (Ferryman to the Underworld)
He's the delivery service of the Underworld, profound, conscientious and precise. This character makes a brief appearance only.
SONGS: (As per Greek Chorus)

Cab Driver
Your stereotypical cabbie. This character makes a brief appearance only, and can be played as a female if required.
SONGS: (As per Greek Chorus)

Daimons
Two of the Daimons have a tiny amount of dialogue: Most Efficient Daimon & Ambitious Daimon. Their character names are description enough, and they can be either male or female.
SONGS: (As per Greek Chorus)

GREEK CHORUS

Ideally, the Greek Chorus should always act as one group, and play as many of the "stage machinery" roles as possible, in full view of the audience. This includes moving, or being, scenery; sound effects, made vocally or with use of mechanical implements; magical effects, etc. However, it's nice to name each individual, and the Greek Alphabet provides many potential names. Other minor Greek Myth character names could be used. (E.g.: the Fates, the Furies, the Muses, the Seasons, etc.) It is possible to split the Greek Chorus into multiple group roles, allowing for many more participants in the show.
SONGS: Swing!; Pandemonium!; Curiosity / Pride / Pestilence / Doubt / Vanity / Greed Will Do That To Ya; Box Speaks No. 1-4; Look At Young Icarus Fly; Moving On; Wildest Dreams; How?; Say That You Love Me; Gold Fever; Some Day; Keep The Faith

Greek Chorus roles include the following:

General: Narrators & Miscellaneous Scenery / Scene Changes / Stage Effects as required

ACT I
Prologue: Mortals on Earth; thunderbolts sound effects
Scene 1: Evils
Scene 2: Bird sound effects
Scene 3: The Voice of The Box
Scene 4.. Icarus flying and crashing
Scene 5: Oarsmen
Scene 6: The Voice of the Box
Scene 8: Oarsmen
Scene 9. Hera's Spell effects
Scene 10: Animals

ACT II
Scene 1: Daimons
Scene 2: Epimetheus' transformation into Zeus
Scene 3: Flowers; Echo's Voice
Scene 4: Dionysus' Spells; Midas' Touch
Scene 5: Daimons (if required)
Scene 6.. The Voice of the Box
Scene 7: Monsters (The Minotaur, Medusa, Scylla)
Scene 8: The Voice of the Box; Hope emerging effects; Monsters

Song Notes

The Prayer
This number introduces the idea that the mortals on Earth have stopped praying to the gods almost entirely, since life on Earth is so perfect that they have no need to ask the immortals for help. It should be sung by as large a group as possible, to heighten the effect of the abrupt ending.

No. 1 Swing!
The "world" of the show can be built in front of the audience during this number, at the same time illustrating the idea of a "world" of theatre and theatrical mechanics. Visually, the journey from a blank stage to a complete set, from actors to characters in costume, could be used to draw the audience into the story. Swing dance moves might add to the party atmosphere of the Wedding that follows.

No. 2 Pandemonium!
The release of Evils into the world is a pivotal moment in this show, and it offers an opportunity to emphasise the contrast between Earth before Evil and Earth after Evil. The Greek Chorus themselves can be used to play the Evils, or they can manipulate an object. For example, they might remove a ribbon from the Box, which they can then pass to the target of that particular Evil so that actor can "wear" their Evil for the remainder of the show. Instead of ribbons, a variety of relevant objects could be used to specifically indicate each Evil.

No. 3 Curiosity Will Do That To Ya
All the "Greek Chorus Comments" should be performed directly to the audience. These are the comments the Greek Chorus makes on the action in the story, and are therefore slightly separate from the rest of the story. This separation can be emphasised using lighting or staging effects.

No. 4 The Box Speaks #1
It should be made visually clear to the audience that the Greek Chorus are portraying a voice coming out of Pandora's Box. This can be achieved simply through performance, if Pandora directs her reactions to the Box alone and never acknowledges the presence of the Greek Chorus, or with use of other indications. For example, the Greek Chorus can use masks to "blank out" their own faces. There should always be a sense of urgency in the Voice of the Box, and song tempos as indicated in the score are vitally important.

No. 5 Look At Young Icarus Fly!
This number can be very easy to stage. A set of steps or a rostrum could be used to give Icarus some height. As Icarus stands on the top step and "flies", the "Crowd" could stand and perform towards the audience, as if they are separate to him, and watching him high above the auditorium. This will give the impression that the two groups are in different places, and the effect is enhanced if Icarus is upstage of the "Crowd". The Greek Chorus could also move the steps or rostrum around on wheels, thus adding to the effect of flying. Alternatively, if the venue allows, the "Crowd" can step down into the auditorium so they are lower than Icarus on stage. If it's safe to do so, Icarus' fall can be achieved by a real fall into the arms of the Greek Chorus. Alternatively, he can "fall" by running down steps, or appear to fall as the "Crowd" runs up to his level onstage. The effects of flying and falling can also be achieved with use of lighting effects, if Icarus and the "Crowd" are lit in separate spaces onstage. Dry ice or cloud effects could be used to enhance the staging of this song. How ever Icarus meets his fate, it's preferable for the effect to be achieved in a "Theatrically Mechanical" way, making full use of the Greek Chorus.

No. 6 Pride Will Do That To Ya
See No. 3.

No. 7 Moving On
See No. 4 for the Greek Chorus' role in this song. Pandora has a moment of realization during this number, and it should be staged as simply as possible, to allow for maximum focus on her dramatic journey.

No. 8 You're The Only One Who's King! (+ Encores)
In contrast to the previous number, this song should be played full of energy and movement. Eros is at his wits' end with Zeus, having spent an eternity trying to make him understand the consequence of his actions. However, the God of Love knows that Zeus is a sucker for a good time, and if he can just engage his King in a song and dance, maybe the message will sink in. Eros works hard in this song, and his dancing and performance should show that hard work to the audience ... but not to Zeus. The King of the Gods is, of course, easily swayed by this technique, and it doesn't take him long to join in with the fun. As soon as he does this, he gets the point ... and then gets a little carried away, as is his wont, which results in the Encores. Although these Encores are somewhat optional, they're based more in Zeus' character than in audience response.

No. 9 Pestilence Will Do That To Ya
See No. 3.

No. 10 Wildest Dreams
During this scene, Epimetheus is inspired by the nature surrounding them, and turns the following things into these animals: a stone—turtle; leaves on the trees—birds; a vine—snake; a shadow—panther; grey thunder clouds—elephants; the river—a crocodile; white fluffy clouds—sheep; flowers—butterflies. This is how Epimetheus was inspired to create animals in the first place, and now he can show Pandora his one passion, his one skill. It's the most exciting moment for him ... even though he thinks Pandora exists only in his imagination. This is his one and only dream. For Pandora, this is a magical moment beyond her wildest dreams ... mostly because she's only had one night in which to dream. The staging for this number can be as simple or as complicated as required. In its simplest form, the animals could be portrayed by the Greek Chorus with use of coloured fabrics, which can be draped over the body to form the animal shape, and give a sense of the colour of each creature. Alternatively, puppets can be made for the animals, and manipulated by the Greek Chorus. The puppets can be hidden behind stones, trees, etc. until they are "created", or they can be constructed to look like a stone, tree, etc., and then be manipulated into their animal form. Shadow puppetry could also be used for this song, and other lighting effects can be used to enhance the image of a "jungle of creation".

No. 11 The Box Speaks #2
See No. 4.

No. 11a Wildest Dreams—Reprise #1
Epimetheus is still afraid of facing Pandora without the protection of his imagination. In this brief moment, he finds the courage to accept that he might be Pandora's Wildest Dream. In considering the freedom with which his animals live their life, he himself finds the freedom to show his love for Pandora.

No. 13 How?
The staging of this journey out of the Underworld does not necessarily require steps. The idea of climbing up to the Earth could be achieved with "walking" and "climbing" dance moves. To make the journey more varied, the Greek Chorus might form tunnels and obstacles through which Orpheus and Eurydice must pass. As Daimons, the Greek Chorus should tempt and torment Orpheus on his journey, attempting to make him turn around. When he does turn, Eurydice can be "dragged back down" to the Underworld by the Daimons. Musically, Orpheus can show the difference between his own inner thoughts during his solo sections, and the effect the Daimons are having on him during their shared sections, by performing the solos with more of a rock style. Lighting effects can be used to emphasise the journey from the darkness of the Underworld towards the light of Earth.

No. 14 Doubt Will Do That To Ya
See No. 3.

No. 15 Stop!
Hera should perform this song in a spoof R&B style, with vocal improvisations if possible. This is her moment to confront Zeus, and she's not letting him get a word in edgeways. Either he has no choice but to be married to her for all eternity, or he really does care about her. Whichever it may be, he's certainly interested in calming her down, and can even grovel a bit in this number. The Heroes should perform this number as spoof R&B backing vocalists, with dance moves to match.

No. 16 Say That You Love Me
This number provides a softer moment. The staging must indicate clearly to the audience that Narcissus is surrounded by flowers, and lingers so long with his own reflection that he grows roots and becomes a flower himself. Towards the very end of the song, when the Greek Chorus become Echo's voice, the staging must indicate clearly to the audience that she has faded away into nothing but a voice, although she doesn't have to disappear from view altogether. This song could be staged so that Narcissus and Echo are on either side of the river, creating a divide between them that cannot be crossed.

No. 17 Vanity Will Do That To Ya
See No. 3.

No. 18 Gold Fever
Midas clearly turns into a Diva at this point in the show, and his song should be performed with a gregarious style. The Greek Chorus can play Disco Queens, and the addition of gold pom-poms, gold sunglasses or other gilded accoutrements may assist this disco image. The turning of Midas into gold can be achieved very simply, with gold fabric or yellow lighting ... or the actor can underdress a gold version of his costume, and tear away the top layer to reveal it as he turns himself into gold.

No. 19 Greed Will Do That To Ya
See No. 3.

No. 20 The "It-Takes-Two-To-Tango" Tango
This number gives Hades the chance to "seduce" Zeus. He (or she) has been waiting for this opportunity for millennia, and now he can get his hands on the Earth as well as the Underworld. He knows he has to play Zeus carefully, but he also knows that Zeus is a sucker for a song and dance. The King of the Gods is an old romantic at heart and has never understood any of Hades'

business ways, no matter how often they're explained to him. This number should be staged as an exaggerated spoof tango, making the most of the comedic visual of the two gods dancing together.

No. 21 The Box Speaks #3
See No. 4.

No. 23 Wildest Dreams—Reprise #2
Epimetheus and Pandora come together and acknowledge their love for one another. This song should be a fairytale moment, during which all thoughts of the Evils and the Box are forgotten. Even by the audience.

No. 24 The Box Speaks #4
See No. 4. At this stage, the Voice in the Box should be more persistent than ever, as it provides an important dramatic build-up to the opening of the Box.

No. 25 Some Day...
This song should be staged simply, and works best with little or no movement at all. Hope emerging from the Box could be staged using imagery such as a rainbow, light, or even a flurry of butterflies, but Hope must appear to emerge from the Box itself.

No. 26 Lullaby
The Heroes have another spoof moment here, as a "boy band", and the comedic value should be emphasised with appropriate "boy band" movement.

No. 27 Keep The Faith
As per indications in the score, this number should begin almost gently, as the characters make their way out of the Labyrinth. The Greek Chorus could be used to provide obstacles such as walls and tunnels, but should gradually disperse during the song. The characters must arrive back at Epimetheus' and Pandora's House, at which time the staging must indicate that they are finally wed. By the end of the number, the audience should feel as if they want to join in with this rousing climax to the show!

Composer's Notes

Musical Interpretation
Metronome markings have been printed in the score to indicate the tempo for each number. In order to recreate the appropriate style for each song it is essential that these are stuck to as closely as possible. Other markings such as dynamics and expression should also be closely regarded. Within these

parameters there is still a lot of scope for interpretation—use of rubato whenever possible, will give the songs a more natural and expressive feel. Principals should be encouraged to put "actor" before "singer" so that the meaning of the song and its relevance to their character and to the plot comes across clearly.

To help interpret and understand the music further, a CD can be borrowed from Samuel French (together with the score) containing all of the main songs in the show. The recording must be used for perusal and learning purposes only and not for playback during a performance.

Scores
The Piano/Conductor/Vocal Score can be hired from Samuel French and provides the full piano accompaniment, chords, vocal lines and lyrics for all the music in the show. The score should be used by the Musical Director in rehearsals and as the "Piano Part" during the performance (see "Instrumentation" below). The score is marked up with instrumental cues so that it can also be used to conduct from.

Vocal Books are also available from Samuel French containing the vocal lines (melodies / harmonies / lyrics etc) for all music in the show. These are intended for the cast (Principals and Greek Chorus) to use during rehearsals.

Instrumentation
The piano forms the core of the instrumentation and must be used in performance—the show can be performed quite effectively with just a piano alone. However, to add interest to the musical accompaniment, other instruments can be added in one of the following combinations:

(i)   Bass guitar *or* Percussion
(ii) Bass guitar *and* Percussion
(iii) Bass guitar *and/or* Percussion *and* Reed I (Flute, Clarinet, Alto Sax) *and* Brass I (Trumpet, Flugel)

Please note in the case of (iii) above, both the Reed and Brass player is required for the arrangement to work.

The Percussion part is written to be played by one person. However, if desired, it could be split into up to three main parts: (a) Drum Kit, (b) Timpani and (c) Glockenspeil. Other percussion instruments e.g. Bell Tree, Tambourine, etc. could be shared out between these players.

In conjunction with one of the above combinations, a Guitar (Electric or

Acoustic) could be added, playing from the chords in the Vocal Score (when appropriate); or a 2nd Keyboard using the Vocal Score as a basis for improvisation, providing extra sounds, effects, etc.

As more instruments are added to the arrangement, the pianist will find that he or she can get away with playing less. Certain parts of the accompaniment, e.g. melodies, melodic fills, bass riffs, etc. should not be doubled by the piano if other instruments are playing them. The instrumental cue markings in the Vocal Score will help the pianist identify these passages.

Band parts and additional Piano/Conductor/Vocal Scores are available for hire from Samuel French.

Set and Properties

A list of the minimum set and properties required for this show can be found at the end of this libretto. Other set and properties can be added according to staging and character requirements.

Costume

Costumes can be simplified according to the available resources. There are many characters in this show, and careful costuming will help the audience identify who is who. Costuming the Greek Chorus in one standard way will assist in their group identity, as well as ease the exchange of groups of Greek Chorus if required. The traditional Ancient Greek "Chiton" can be used, but the show can be costumed in any historical era up to modern day. Suggestions for use of costume as identification:
* Use of colour-coding to identify the character pairs (e.g.: gold for Zeus and Hera, purple for Pandora and Epimetheus, blue for Daedalus and Icarus, green for Narcissus and Echo, yellow for Dionysus and Midas, orange for Orpheus and Eurydice, red for Eros, black for Hades, white for the Greek Chorus).
* Use of patterns to identify the individual characters (e.g.: animal prints for Epimetheus, hearts for Eros, currency symbols for Midas, grapes for Dionysus, musical notes for Orpheus, etc.).

Lighting and Sound Effects

Suggestions for basic lighting can be found at the end of this libretto. This generic lighting plot is a general guide only, and should be enhanced according to available resources and artistic requirements.

The Greek Chorus should make all of the sound effects if they can, either vocally or with an instrument or other mechanism. If performed this way, additional effects cues may be added as required to enhance the role of the Greek Chorus. However, the effects can be pre-recorded if absolutely necessary, and a list of basic effects cues for this purpose can be found at the end of this libretto.

Staging

Despite requiring several different settings, this show should ideally be very simply staged. The Greek Chorus should play as much of the scenery as possible, with the assistance of props and perhaps costume. Lighting effects can also be used to add the appropriate atmosphere for the location. The set could give a suggestion of Ancient Greece if required, but the physical period of this piece is deliberately open to interpretation. A basic set could be erected during **No. 1 Swing!** to emphasize the building of the "theatrical world" of the piece. This can consist of anything from Greek columns to scaffolding or rostra. The option of different levels will be useful for staging certain scenes. Please note that scene changes must be simple and fast, in order to maintain the fast pace of this show. Music is specifically allotted in the score, either during the "Greek Chorus Comment" songs or in scene change music.

The basic scenic locations required for this show are as follows (with staging suggestions):

Mount Olympus—could be defined by use of a projected image of Earth from outer space, thus allowing for any area of the stage to be used in these scenes. During **The Prayer**, the Greek Chorus could stand behind a gauze through which they can be seen by the audience, to separate Earth from Mount Olympus. Raised levels could also be used for Mount Olympus, but they do limit movement space. A throne for Zeus and Hera could also be used to indicate that this is the home of the gods.

A bare stage—upon which the main show is built during **No.1 Swing!**.

Inside Epimetheus' House on Earth—a defined entrance such as steps or a doorway could be used to emphasise Pandora's entrance. Balloons and other decorations might give the scene a visual party atmosphere. The Greek Chorus could play statues around the house, frozen in position when they're not addressing the audience.

Outside Epimetheus' House on Earth—the Greek Chorus might play a fountain, using strips of blue silk for water. They could also hold small bird puppets, or play trees behind which the characters can look for Pandora.

A River—this could be one long strip of blue silk that can be moved to different positions on the stage to represent a different area of river. If a set of steps is placed under the silk at one end, it might represent a waterfall. During these scenes, the Greek Chorus play oarsmen, or flowers, but they could also play trees and surrounding vegetation.

The Woods—the Greek Chorus should play trees in the woods, reacting to Dionysus' wind and heat spells. Lighting effects can be used to enhance the atmosphere with the image of dappled light through the trees.

The Underworld—This should be represented in a modern way to give the idea of an efficient office, but the more traditional use of lighting effects to create images of flame could complement the setting. Hades' desk is his throne, and should be impressive. The Greek Chorus play Daimons in the Underworld, but they could also play Hades' desk and chair!

Outside the Labyrinth—a clear entrance should be indicated. The Greek Chorus could play statues defining the entrance.

Inside the Labyrinth—The Greek Chorus could be used to define the twists and turns inside the maze. Strips of muslin or cloth could also be hung to indicate the divisions inside. If muslin cloth is used, characters winding or fighting their way through will be seen more clearly.

There are variations on, and combinations of, these locations listed in the main script.

With thanks to our Directors, Julia Burgess and Ellie Jones, and to all our fantastic cast members, for their invaluable assistance in the exploration and development of this show.

MUSICAL NUMBERS

PROLOGUE

The Prayer — Greek Chorus

ACT I

No. 1	**Swing!**	Full Company
No. 1a-1f	Introductions	
No. 1g-1i	Fanfares	
No. 2	**Pandemonium!**	Zeus & Full Company
No. 2a-2g	Evil Musical Stings	
No. 3	**Curiosity Will Do That To Ya**	Greek Chorus
No. 4	**The Box Speaks #1**	Greek Chorus
No. 5	**Look At Young Icarus Fly!**	Daedalus, Icarus, Characters & Greek Chorus
No. 5a	Scene Change and Underscore	
No. 5b	Charon	
No. 6	**Pride Will Do That To Ya**	Greek Chorus
No. 7	**Moving On**	Pandora & Greek Chorus
No. 7a	Scene Change	
No. 8	**You're The Only One Who's King!**	Eros & Zeus
No. 8a	**Enc. #1—You're The Only One Who's King!**	Eros & Zeus
No. 8b	**Enc. #2—You're The Only One Who's King!**	Eros & Zeus
No. 8c	Scene Change	
No. 8d	Charon	
No. 9	**Pestilence Will Do That To Ya**	Greek Chorus
No. 9a	Hera's Spell	
No. 9b	Scene Change	
No. 10	**Wildest Dreams**	Epimetheus, Pandora & Greek Chorus
No. 11	**The Box Speaks #2**	Greek Chorus
No. 11a	**Wildest Dreams (Reprise #1)**	Epimetheus

ACT II

No. 12	Entr'acte	
No. 13	**How?**	Orpheus & Greek Chorus
No. 14	**Doubt Will Do That To Ya**	Greek Chorus
No. 15	**Stop!**	Hera & Heroes
No. 15a	Scene Change	
No. 16	**Say That You Love Me**	Narcissus, Echo & Greek Chorus
No. 17	**Vanity Will Do That To Ya**	Greek Chorus
No. 17a-17c	Dionysus' Spells	
No. 18	**Gold Fever**	Midas & Greek Chorus
No. 19	**Greed Will Do That To Ya**	Greek Chorus
No. 20	**The "It-Takes-Two-To-Tango" Tango**	Hades & Zeus
No. 20a	Scene Change	
No. 21	**The Box Speaks #3**	Greek Chorus
No. 22	The Battle	
No. 23	**Wildest Dreams (Reprise #2)**	Epimetheus & Pandora
No. 24	**The Box Speaks #4**	Greek Chorus
No. 25	**Some Day…**	Characters & Greek Chorus
No. 25a	The Battle (Reprise)	
No. 26	**Lullaby**	Heroes
No. 26a	Exit of Monsters	
No. 27	**Keep The Faith!**	Full Company
No. 27a	Calls	
No. 28	**Keep The Faith! (Reprise)**	Full Company
No. 28a	Exit Music	

SYNOPSIS OF SCENES

PROLOGUE

Zeus and Hera (Mount Olympus)

ACT I

The Opening (Onstage at The Theatre)
SCENE 1   The Wedding (Earth, Inside Epimetheus' House)
SCENE 2   Where Did She Go? (Outside the House)
SCENE 3   Pandora and Zeus (Outside the House)
SCENE 4   Daedalus and Icarus (Outside the House)
SCENE 5   Icarus and Charon (A River)
SCENE 6   Pandora et al (The Same River)
SCENE 7   Zeus and Eros (Mount Olympus)
SCENE 8   Eurydice Dies (A Part of the River in the Woods)
SCENE 9   Hera and Echo (The Same Part of the River)
SCENE 10   Pandora and Epimetheus (The Same Part of the River)

ACT II

SCENE 1   Orpheus in the Underworld (The Underworld)
SCENE 2   Which One's Epimetheus? (The Woods)
SCENE 3   Echo and Narcissus (A Flowery Part of the River)
SCENE 4   Midas and Dionysus (In The Woods)
SCENE 5   Zeus and Hades (The Underworld)
SCENE 6   Epimetheus and Eros (Outside the Labyrinth)
SCENE 7   Monsters! (Inside the Labyrinth)
SCENE 8   Hope (In the Very Centre of the Labyrinth)
SCENE 9   Out of the Labyrinth and Back to the House

ACKNOWLEDGEMENTS

Pandemonium! (a Greek Myth-adventure) was originally developed at New York University's Tisch School of the Arts in the Graduate Musical Theatre Writing Program.

Jenifer and David would like to thank the following people for their continuing support:

In New York
Mindi Dickstein
Karen Henderson
Robert Lee
Chris Miller
Nathan Tysen
Cycle X
Sarah Schlesinger and the faculty of the
Graduate Musical Theatre Writing Program
Dean Mary Schmidt Campbell of Tisch School of the Arts, NYU

In Guildford
James Barber and The Yvonne Arnaud Theatre, Guildford
The ACT 2 kids (and their parents!)
Julia Burgess

In Continuous Development Everywhere
Ellie Jones
The Lovely John Harris

In General
Simon Pearsall
Our families and loved ones

For Julia & Ellie

Other titles by Jenifer Toksvig and David Perkins
published by Samuel French Ltd

The Curious Quest for the Sandman's Sand
Shake Ripple & Roll
Skool & Crossbones

PANDEMONIUM! (A GREEK MYTH-ADVENTURE)

PROLOGUE

Zeus and Hera. (Mount Olympus)

Mount Olympus can be a space separated from the main setting by light, height or scenery

The set should be easily manipulated by the Greek Chorus in view of the audience. They are the "Deus Ex Machina". The more theatrically mechanical the scenery the better. The Greek Chorus should also make as many of the sound effects as possible, in view of the audience

The Greek Chorus are the mortals on Earth. They pray to Zeus, who is watching them from Mount Olympus

The Prayer

Greek Chorus (Mortals) Oh Zeus, oh Zeus, oh Zeus, oh Zeus, oh Zeus!
We mortals offer thanks to you from one and all.
You made the Earth spectacular. We have a ball.
So thanks a lot. What a guy. (What a guy!)
That's it. See you next year. Goodbye!

Zeus That's it? Last year it was at least an hour long! And one dried-up old goat does not make a sacrifice! (*He throws a thunderbolt down to Earth*) Nobody appreciates me. I made it too perfect down there. Typical Hades... "Oh no, Brother, I don't mind torturing the dead and living in the Underworld. You take the perfect Earth." Now I just give, give, give and what thanks do I get? (*He pauses*) Hmm. Maybe it's time for one more gift from the gods. (*A thunderclap as Zeus magics a Box from thin air*) Let's see if the perfect Earth likes this little present...

Hera enters

Zeus hides the Box from her

Hera Is that a wedding present for Epimetheus, Zeus? You already gave him a bride, and all he did was make some smelly animals for Earth.
Zeus This isn't for Epimetheus, Hera.
Hera Oh? Who's it for then? (*She preens*)
Zeus No-one! Shouldn't you be going down? The wedding's about to start.
Hera Zeus, what are you up to?
Zeus I'm not up to anything! I'm just trying to run the universe and rule over good. What ever happened to trust?!
Hera Whatever happened to respect?!

Hera exits

Zeus Women! (*To Earth*) Mortals! (*To the Box*) Evil... (*He summons Hermes*)

Hermes, the messenger, enters

Zeus hands him the Box

Take this to Epimetheus and Pandora's wedding. And ... umm ... it's a surprise, so don't tell them I sent you, there's a good chap.
Hermes Righto, guv'nor.

Hermes exits

Zeus laughs, and exits in the other direction

ACT I

The Opening

Onstage at the Theatre

The Company appears in this song as the Company, not as Characters or Greek Chorus. During the song they could set up the props and scenery, and perhaps put on costumes that indicate their characters in view of the audience. As they sing, Hermes arrives on Earth to deliver the Box. He places it with other wedding gifts already in place

No. 1 Swing!

Company Welcome to the world!
Everybody cheer!
Come on in and celebrate
The wedding of the year!
Come and meet the gods!
Come and see the show!
Will there be a tale or two
To tell before we go?

C'mon swing! Let's celebrate!
C'mon swing! Oo wa!
C'mon swing! Let's celebrate!
C'mon swing! Oo wa!
Jus' clap your hands 'cause swingin' is the thing!

Will you see a god?
Will you see a king?
Who will be the next in line
To join us in the swing?
Will they bring a gift
Tied up with a bow?
Will there be a tale or two
To tell before we go?

C'mon swing! Let's celebrate!

C'mon swing! Oo wa!
C'mon swing! Let's celebrate!
C'mon swing! Oo wa!
Jus' clap your hands 'cause swingin' is the thing!

Instrumental dance break

C'mon swing! Let's celebrate! C'mon swing! Oo wa!
C'mon swing! Let's celebrate! C'mon swing! Oo wa!
Jus' clap your hands 'cause swingin' is the thing!
Jus' clap your hands 'cause swingin' is the thing!
Jus' clap your hands 'cause swingin' is the...
The swing is the thing!

By this point, the Company are now the Characters or the Greek Chorus, and should act accordingly

The Lights cross-fade to:

Scene 1

The Wedding. (Earth, Inside Epimetheus' House)

The following scene of dialogue should be set as if the audience is overhearing snippets of conversation in the crowd of guests at the wedding party ... with the exception of their name introductions to the audience

The Greek Chorus are distanced from the crowd, and speak to the audience through the scene

Epimetheus and Eros are first. Epimetheus is wearing glasses (**Music 1a**)

Eros Eros!
Greek Chorus The god of love!
Epimetheus Epimetheus!
Greek Chorus Creator of the animals!
Eros Epimefeus! Ready to tie the old knot, guv?
Epimetheus Eros, I can't find my glasses...
Eros They're on the end of your nose.
Epimetheus Ah, thank you. Where's Pandora?
Eros Trying to learn everything about the entire universe in one day.
Epimetheus Gosh!
Eros Oh, she'll be fine. I gave her a book. (**Music 1b**)

Act I, Scene 1

We focus on Echo and Narcissus. Narcissus carries a large hand-mirror. Echo carries a smaller version of the same. As they speak, they place these gifts with the others

Narcissus Narcissus!
Greek Chorus The most beautiful mortal on Earth!
Echo Echo!
Greek Chorus Nymph of the woods!
Narcissus So anyway, Zeus said to Epimetheus, "I've made you a wife and the wedding's tomorrow!" Can you believe it!
Echo Narcissus! Don't tell tales!
Narcissus But I heard that Zeus made Pandora out of clay!
Echo I bet she's gorgeous.
Narcissus Not as gorgeous as you are, Echo. (**Music 1c**)

We focus on Dionysus and Midas. Dionysus has a flask of wine. Midas has a pouch of coins. As they speak, they place these items with the other gifts

Dionysus Dionysus!
Greek Chorus God of wine!
Midas King Midas!
Greek Chorus Ruler of Phrygia!
Midas I thought wine was only for sacrifices, Dionysus?
Dionysus That's right! It's my wedding present. Finest sacrificial wine! What've you got them?
Midas Couldn't decide, so I'm just giving them lots of money! (**Music 1d**)

We focus on Daedalus and Icarus. Daedalus is carrying a white feather quill. As he speaks, he places it with the other gifts

Daedalus Daedalus!
Greek Chorus Mortal architect, famed for the Labyrinth, inventor of the saw!
Icarus Icarus!
Greek Chorus His son!
Icarus Wow! Look at this house! Did you really build it, Dad?
Daedalus Aye, reckon it came out all right...
Icarus I'm going to build houses like this!

Icarus runs off

Daedalus Icarus! You have to learn how to walk before you can fly, you know! That boy'll be the death of me... (**Music 1e**)

We focus on Orpheus and Eurydice. Orpheus is carrying a small lyre, which he places with the other wedding gifts

Orpheus Orpheus!
Greek Chorus The greatest musician on Earth!
Eurydice Eurydice!
Greek Chorus His most adored and adorable wife!
Orpheus Hey, Eurydice, I want you to meet… (*he spots Eros*) some of the guys!
Eros Orpheus! 'Allo, mate! Gonna play us some music?
Orpheus Later, man, yeah. Hey Eros, meet Eurydice. She puts the mellow in my melody, the core in my chords, she puts the muse in the musician. Yeah.
Eurydice And you're my guiding star.
Orpheus Follow me, babe.
Eurydice To Hades and back, Orpheus!
Orpheus Yeah, it's gonna be a hell of a night…

Eurydice and Orpheus wander off into the crowd

Eros watches them go

Eros Can you feel the love tonight? (**Music 1f**)

We focus on Theseus, Odysseus and Perseus. Theseus is wearing a ridiculous red woolly jumper

Theseus Theseus!
Odysseus Odysseus!
Perseus Perseus!
Greek Chorus Brave and daring heroes of Earth!
Perseus New jumper, Theseus?
Theseus Yes, Perseus!
Odysseus ⎱ (*together*) Ohhh…
Perseus ⎰
Theseus Made to measure!
Perseus ⎱ (*together*) Ohhh…
Odysseus ⎰
Theseus Completely weapon-proof!
Perseus ⎱ (*together*) Ohhh…
Odysseus ⎰
Odysseus Where'd you get it?
Theseus My mum made it.
Odysseus ⎱ (*together*) Oh. (**Music 1g**)
Perseus ⎰

Act I, Scene 1   7

Eros Gods and goddesses, nymphs and mortals, please welcome ... the groom, Epimetheus!

Epimetheus steps forward, looking slightly uncomfortable. The Crowd cheers and claps loudly. Epimetheus speaks over the noise

Epimetheus (*whispering loudly*) Eros! I can't find my speech!
Eros Wot?
Epimetheus I can't find my speech!
Eros Wot?!

The Crowd stops cheering and clapping

Epimetheus (*shouting at first*) I can't find my sp...eople of Olympus and Earth! Gods and Goddesses, nymphs and mortals ... err ... welcome! Thanks for coming along at such short notice. You're probably wondering what the blushing bride looks like, aren't you?

There's General Muttering in the Crowd...

   Yes, well ... so am I. Eros? (**Music 1h**)
Eros Epimefeus, may I present your bride... Pandora!

Pandora enters

There is a collective gasp from the Crowd

Epimetheus (*obviously impressed*) Gosh, umm... (*gulp*) ... Yes... Err...
Eros (*prompting Epimetheus*) Hello!
Epimetheus Hello! I'm Epimetheus.
Pandora Hello, E-pi-me-the-us. It's very nice to eat you!
Eros (*whispering to Pandora*) Meet!
Pandora It's very nice to eat meat! (**Music 1i**)
Eros No, no, no...
Greek Chorus Hera, Queen of the gods!

Hera enters

Everyone except Epimetheus and Pandora turns to Hera and bows or curtsies. Epimetheus is unable to take his eyes off Pandora. Neither of them noticed Hera's entrance. (How cute is that?)

Hera Epimetheus, darling!
Epimetheus (*to Pandora*) Pandora...

Eros Epimetheus!
Epimetheus Pandora...
Eros Epimetheus!
Epimetheus Pandora...
Eros ⎫
Hera ⎭ (*together*) Epimetheus!!
Epimetheus Hera! Ah! Welcome to Earth! Right ... speech... First of all, I'd like to thank everyone for their generous gifts. Poseidon had an urgent storm in the Mediterranean, but he sent some lovely halibut... (*He continues ad lib silently*)

Epimetheus and the Crowd fade into the background, leaving Pandora in an innocent reverie amongst the gifts

Pandora He's so ... oh! He's just ... what's the word? And look at all these lovely things! I wonder what this is for? And this one? Oh, look at this! (*She picks up the Box*) It's so pretty! What is it?

The Lights cross-fade to blue/green

No. 2 Pandemonium

I think there's something inside it.

Pause for music

I'll just peek...

Pause for music

How do you open it up? (*She tries to figure out how to open the lid*)

Zeus watches, and sings to the contents of the Box

Zeus Na na-na na Na na-na na Na na-na na na na na Come out of the Box for Daddy now. Na na-na na na na na You know it's time to feed. Na na-na na na na na Raging Thirst, do your worst!	**Greek Chorus (Evils)** Oo... Oo...

Act I, Scene 1

Na na-na na na na na
Bug-eyed Greed, give me what I
 need!

Panic. Hate. Don't you make me
 wait!
Hey Jealousy! Don't you wanna
 be free?

Pandora opens the Box. (That would be her first mistake.) The Evils (Greek Chorus) fly into the room

Zeus It's pandemonium! (Haha ha
 ha!)

 It's pandemonium!

Evils Oo-wa-oo bop bop

 Oo-wa-oo bop bop
 Oo-wa-oo...
 Oo-wa-oo...
 Oo-wa-oo...

Zeus It's pandemonium! (Haha ha
 ha!)

 It's pandemonium!

Evils Oo-wa-oo bop bop

 Oo-wa-oo bop bop
 Oo-wa-oo...
 Oo-wa-oo...
 Oo-wa-oo...

Zeus It's pandemonium! (Haha ha
 ha!)

 It's pandemonium!

Instrumental break

All What's that wicked beat?
 It's pandemonium!

 What's that wicked beat?
 It's pandemonium!
Characters
Pandora (*together*) Something
 crazy in the air.
 I can feel it ev'rywhere.
 Start to shiver. Start to shake.
 Ain't no party.
 It ain't no piece of cake.
All What's that wicked beat?
 It's pandemonium!

 What's that wicked beat?
 It's pandemonium!
Characters
Pandora (*together*) Is it
 poison? Is it doom?
 Are there sirens in the room?
 Are the furies in my head?
 Are the fates
 About to cut my thread?
All What's that wicked beat?
 It's pandemonium!

 What's that wicked beat?
 It's pandemonium!

Zeus Na na-na na na na na
  Arrogance and Vanity!   (*Alt.*) Arrogance!
  Paranoid Insanity!   (*Alt.*) Vanity!
  Na na-na na na na na
  Blasphemous Profanity!   (*Alt.*) Insanity!
  Bring it on!

  Na na-na na na na na
  Calamity gregarious!   (*Alt.*) Calamity!
  Depravity nefarious!   (*Alt.*) Depravity!
  Na na-na na na na na
  Morality precarious!   (*Alt.*) Morality!
  Hear my song!

  An eruption of corruption   **Evils** Oo...
  Is the way to make them pay.   Oo...
  Gotta suspicion   Oo...
  The human condition
  Is gonna make my day!   Oo... Wah!
                                       All What's that wicked beat?
  It's pandemonium! (You   It's pandemonium!
    betchya, baby!)
                                       What's that wicked beat?
  It's pandemonium!   It's pandemonium!

The song crescendos into a mad cacophony, faster and faster, until the moment we see each evil actually enter its chosen victim. Pandora has, by now, realized that something's not quite right

The following singing overlaps

Zeus   Na na-na na (*Repeat 4 times*)
               Ha-ha ha ha ha!
Greek Chorus (Evils) Oo... (*Repeat 8 times*)
Characters ⎫
               ⎬ (*together*) Oh Zeus! (*Repeat 8 times*)
Pandora   ⎭

On the last beat of the song, Pandora forces the lid shut, abruptly ending the madness—and Zeus' insane laughter. She holds the Box, shut tight. The Lights snap to a general state. The Characters are unaware of events in the song, and resume the positions they were in before the Box was opened. They listen to Epimetheus as if nothing has happened. Zeus continues to watch from Mount Olympus

Act I, Scene 1

Epimetheus And finally, we'll be making a sacrifice to all the——

Dionysus interrupts him loudly. The musical "stings" could be used to register the group's and individuals' reaction to the words spoken. As they speak, some (or all) of them take back their wedding gifts and keep them as personal props. Dionysus picks up his flask of wine

Dionysus Yes, let's make a sacrifice! Anyone fancy a drink? (**Music 2a**)
Odysseus I have the best iron sword!
Perseus I have the best bronze shield!
Theseus I have the best woolly jumper! (**Music 2b**)
Daedalus Let's take a tour around my house!
Icarus Dad! It's not your house! (**Music 2c**)
Eurydice I've got tummy ache. Maybe I should go home.
Orpheus Don't, like, leave me here alone, babe! (**Music 2d**)
Midas What was I thinking, giving them all this money? It's mine! (*He takes back his money.* **Music 2e**)
Echo Tell me some gossip, Narcissus!
Narcissus Who cares about gossip? Let's talk about me. (**Music 2f**)
Pandora Umm ... what was that? (**Music 2g**)
Midas That was the groom's speech.
Dionysus Anyone would think you were born yesterday!

Midas and Dionysus laugh loudly at their own joke

Eros Midas!
Midas I think Zeus should have made you into a Greek urn.
Pandora What's a Greek urn?
Dionysus About twenty quid a week!

The two men laugh loudly again, joined by others

Pandora Didn't anyone see what was in this Box?
Hera Hey, who gave you that?
Echo What's in it?
Midas Is it money?!
Narcissus Is it a picture of me?
Midas I'll give you five gold pieces for the Box!
Dionysus Midas! Don't be ridiculous!
Midas You're right. Make that four gold pieces!

The two men laugh loudly again

Pandora No, please listen. When I opened the Box...

Echo I think we should all see inside it!
Hera I want to know who it's from! Open the Box!
Midas Four gold pieces! Take the money!

Some join Hera, others Midas, alternating as necessary until Pandora exits

The following speeches overlap

Hera } *(together)* Open the box! *(Repeat)*
Crowd

Midas } *(together)* Take the money! *(Repeat)*
Crowd

Eros All right, that's enough! Stop it this minute! Everyone just stop! *(Repeat ad lib)*
Epimetheus Stop it! Leave her alone, would you? Eros, do something! *(Repeat ad lib)*
Pandora Please! Just listen! All these things came out ... listen ... please, stop! No, please, stop shouting! Oh!

Pandora panics and runs off with the Box

Epimetheus Pandora!

Epimetheus runs off after her

Theseus I'll get her!

Theseus runs entirely the wrong way at first

Odysseus } *(together)* I'll get her!
Perseus

Theseus Wait for me!
All *(rushing off)* Pandora! Come back! *(Etc. ad lib)*

All exit after Pandora

Zeus is still on Mount Olympus

Zeus She saw the evils come out of the Box! But how? No-one else saw them. Don't panic, Zeus, don't panic. Got to hide the evidence. Go down there, get the Box and find out what she saw. Oh...lympus!

Zeus exits

Act I, Scene 2   13

The Lights go down on Olympus. The Greek Chorus change the scenery as they sing the next number

No. 3 Curiosity Will Do That To Ya

Greek Chorus Everybody knows
How the story goes.
Now there ain't no turning back.
If she'd only known the fact that
Curiosity will do that to ya.
Curiosity will do that to ya.

The Lights cross-fade to a general state

Scene 2

Where Did She Go? (Outside the House)

Epimetheus enters, urgently looking for Pandora

All the guests follow him on, looking everywhere

Epimetheus Pandora!?
Everyone (*variously*) Pandora!? / Where are you? / Come back, Pandora! (*Ad lib*)

Everyone looks for her, calling her name and talking, until Eurydice silences them

Eurydice Please don't shout!

Everyone stops talking

I've got a really bad headache. Look, Pandora's probably just scared, and she can't have gone far. I think we should all spread out and find her.
Eros Yes! Thank you.
Narcissus Why would I want to look for a silly girl?
Epimetheus That's my wife you're talking about!
Narcissus No, I'm talking about me.
Echo Well, technically, she is silly to run away from her destiny as decreed by Zeus himself, i.e. to marry Epimetheus and live in a lovely house happily ever after...

Midas Never mind all that! What about the Box?!

Everyone speaks all at once, as follows

Narcissus If it gets me some attention, I want that Box!
Echo Yes, I would like to know what's inside that Box.
Orpheus Maybe she, like, hasn't run off with the Box?
Midas I want the gold in that Box!
Dionysus Did someone say something about a Box?
Eros Something happened with that Box!
Hera I want to know who gave her that Box!
Heroes I'll find the Box!
Theseus No, I'll find the Box!

End of overlap

Eurydice (*interrupting and silencing them*) Please... don't... shout! Come on, Orpheus. Let's go and look for her.
Orpheus (*following Eurydice off*) Or we could just, like, stay here... or go home... or, yeah, we could, like, look for Pandora, or reflect on the whole, like, meaning of the Box thing...

Eurydice exits and Orpheus follows

Everyone else wanders around, looking for Pandora and chatting amongst themselves. We focus on Epimetheus and Eros

Epimetheus Eros, was it something I said?
Eros No, guv, you did great.
Epimetheus But I said "Pandora, Pandora, Pandora..." (*He groans*) I should have said... "Nice dress" or "Hey there, babe"... or... I don't know...
Eros Look, you can't hurry love...

Hera pushes past them

Hera Out of my way! I'm going to find Zeus. I bet he knows exactly where Pandora is.
Eros Wait for me, Hera. I've got a few words for Zeus n'all. Why don't you go 'ome, guv, in case she comes back?
Epimetheus Home. Yes. Right. (*He moves to exit*) "Pandora, I look at you and I think of the elephant!" No, no, no...

Hera and Eros exit one way, Epimetheus another

Act I, Scene 2   15

We focus on Midas and Dionysus

Midas Pandora?!
Dionysus Pandora?!
Midas There's gold in that there Box. I can smell it. Pandora?!
Dionysus A mist of mellow fruitfulness that teases the nose with a saucy hint of summer berries and the warm piquancy of cinnamon...
Midas Dionysus.
Dionysus Sorry. Pandora?!
Midas Pandora?! (*Etc.*)

Midas and Dionysus exit

We focus on Echo and Narcissus

Echo Pandora?! (*Beat*) Someone should tell Zeus about Pandora, you know, because I bet she wasn't supposed to run away like that and I bet he could tell us what's in that Box and... Narcissus? Are you listening to me?

The Heroes leap forward

Odysseus I am looking for Pandora!
Perseus I am looking for Pandora!
Theseus I am looking very smart in my woolly jumper!

The Heroes exit

Narcissus (*towards Theseus*) I'd look better in it.

Narcissus wanders aimlessly off

Echo Narcissus! Wait for me!

Echo runs off after Narcissus

We focus on Daedalus and Icarus. Bird sounds are heard overhead

Icarus Pandora?! Pandora?!
Daedalus Icarus! (*He pauses*) Icarus! I've got it! The birds could spot Pandora from the air!
Icarus Birds can't talk, Dad.
Daedalus But you can...!
Icarus Oh no...

Daedalus If we can find enough feathers, and a few other things, I could make you some wings, Icarus! Bigger and better than any bird! You could fly up into the sky, higher and higher and...
Icarus I can't do that! Are you mad?
Daedalus Nonsense, you can do anything! (*He moves to exit*) Come on! We need some long sticks, some wax, and some feathers...
Icarus Dad, this is such a bad idea...

Daedalus and Icarus exit

Scene 3

Pandora and Zeus. (Outside the House)

Zeus enters, looking for Pandora, who enters from another direction, or perhaps from a hiding place

During their conversation, Zeus does everything he can to take the Box from her—but she turns away from him each time he reaches for it

Zeus Pandora!
Pandora Zeus! I'm so glad to see you! At the wedding, I opened this present because that's what you do with presents, right? And things came out of it, which was OK but then the things sort of made everyone be different... well, maybe not different, I don't know, but it was all ... anyway, I ran away because I was ... well, it wasn't what you said would happen. So, what's in the Box?
Zeus What Box?
Pandora This Box!
Zeus Nothing! Nothing at all! You must have imagined it.

No. 4 The Box Speaks #1

Pandora What does "imagined" mean?
Zeus It means you saw something that wasn't there...

A voice comes from 'inside' the Box—sung by the Greek Chorus

Greek Chorus Set me free...
Pandora What was that?
Zeus What was what?
Greek Chorus Set me free...

Act I, Scene 3

Pandora Did you hear that?
Zeus Now you're hearing things that aren't there...
Pandora No. No, I'm not. There's a voice coming out of the Box.
Greek Chorus All you have to do is set me free.
    Everything will be OK
    If only you believe.
Zeus There's nothing there! Just give me the Box and forget about it!
Pandora Why won't you believe me?
Zeus Look ... it's just that ... you see ... Pandora, there are some things you're just not meant to know.

Pandora and Zeus become more and more agitated

Pandora I know things came out of this Box.
Zeus Things did not come out of it!
Pandora I saw things come out of it!
Zeus Nothing came out!
Pandora Things came out!
Zeus Bad things did not come out of the Box!
Pandora Bad things?
Zeus Look, it's got nothing to do with you, now give me that, you silly girl!
    (*He tries to grab the Box*)

Pandora moves away

Pandora You made me! Aren't you supposed to help me?
Zeus I will help you, just give me that Box!
Pandora No! I don't believe you. Stay away from me!

Pandora runs off with the Box

Zeus Pandora! Women! There must be an evil left in the Box. (*He pauses*) Well, she won't tell anyone ... what could she tell them, anyway? That bad things came out of the Box and she thinks I had something to do with it? (*Beat*) That bad things came out of the Box and she thinks I had something to do with it! If the mortals find out I've been spreading evil around, they won't even pray once a year! Oh no. What if they stop believing in me? I'm doomed!

Zeus runs off

Scene 4

Daedalus and Icarus. (Outside the House)

Daedalus and the Crowd (Midas, Dionysus, Echo, Narcissus, Orpheus, Eurydice and The Heroes) enter, looking offstage as if Icarus is far away, ready for flight

Daedalus shouts offstage when he's talking to Icarus

Daedalus Right, Icarus! Just run as fast as you can for a bit and then hold your arms out and jump! Stand well back, everyone. Nice and fast, Icarus!
Icarus (*off*) What do I do when I've jumped?!
Daedalus You'll get the hang of it in no time! You're a genius! (*Aside*) He's a genius. (*To Icarus*) Ready?

No. 5 Look At Young Icarus Fly!

Icarus (*off*) No!
Daedalus Run!

The Crowd (Characters and Greek Chorus) 'watches' Icarus as if he were running far away

(*Singing*) Faster, faster!
        Icarus It's never gonna work, Dad!
(*Shouting*) Come on, Icarus!
Faster, faster!
        It's never gonna work, Dad!
Faster, faster...
        It's never gonna work, Dad   **Crowd**
Faster, faster...   Come...
        It's never gonna work, Dad   ...On!
Faster, faster...
                                                          Come...
        It's never gonna work, Dad   ...On!
Faster, faster!   Never gonna, never gonna...   There
There he...   Never gonna, never gonna...   He
...Goes!   Oh...!   Goes!

Instrumental break—Icarus enters, now with wings. The Greek Chorus make him fly

Icarus (*shouting*) Dad! I'm flying!

Act I, Scene 4

Daedalus	Look what I've done!
	I've created a miracle!
	Soar like a bird in the sky!
	I knew you could do it!
	Go higher, my son!
	Just look at young Icarus fly!
Icarus	Look where I am!
	It's too scary for words.
	All I see is the ground racing by!
	My father's a nut!
	Do I look like a bird?
	And I really don't know how to fly!
	I really don't know how to fly!
Orpheus	Higher and higher! I wish it were me!
Midas	Just think of the riches I'd suddenly see!
Echo	The top of the clouds where the gods run and play!
Eurydice	The road where the night chases after the day!
Perseus	From so high I could plan out a route of attack!
Odysseus	I would fly across oceans and never look back!
Theseus	I would soar! I would swoop! I would loop the loop!
Crowd	Flying high!
	Just look at young Icarus fly!
Daedalus	Look at the sky!
	How it welcomes you home!
	It's enough to bring tears to the eye!
	Why hover so low?
(*Speaking*)	Fly up higher, my son!
	Just look at young Icarus fly!
Icarus	What did you say?
	Should I fly to the sun?
	It's hot when you're up here so high!
	The brakes are not working!
	I haven't been trained!
	And I really don't know how to fly!
	I really don't know how to fly!
Orpheus	Higher and higher! I'm glad it's not me!
Midas	Just think of the heights I would suddenly see!
Echo	The top of the clouds is a bit far away.
Eurydice	He might be too high now, wouldn't you say?
Perseus	Way up high I might feel a bit sick in the air.
Odysseus	I'd be a bit lonely if I were up there.
Theseus	I'd be scared! I'd come down!
	I would land on the ground!

Crowd He's too high!
Just look at young Icarus fly!
Daedalus Fly up higher and higher and higher and higher...
Daedalus ⎫ (*together*) ...And higher and higher and higher and higher...
Crowd ⎬ ...And higher and higher and higher and higher...
Icarus ⎭
Daedalus ⎫ (*together*) ...And higher and higher and higher and higher
Crowd ⎬ and...
Icarus ⎭
Icarus ...Higher and higher...
(*Speaking*) Dad? Everyone's so far away...

Can this be right?
All the wax has been melting...
My feathers are starting to fry...
Daedalus What's going on?
Now he's losing some height
But I really don't understand why.

Helios—the Sun—has melted the wax on Icarus' wings. (Just a little bit of extra myth-info for you.) As he begins to fall, Daedalus and the Crowd call out to him

Icarus I'm getting too hot...
Daedalus Too close to the sun!
Icarus ...And I'm starting to fall!
Daedalus Is he starting to fall?
Crowd He's starting to fall!
He's starting to fall!
He's falling, falling, falling,   **Daedalus** Icarus!
Falling, falling, falling!   **Icarus** Father!
Crowd (*variously*) No! He's too   **Daedalus** No! Icarus! My son!
young to die! He's falling! He's   Icarus!
out of control! He's going to crash!
What happened?! (*Etc. ad lib*)

Icarus falls from the sky

Perseus He landed over there!
Odysseus By the river!
Theseus Come on!

Everyone runs towards the river as the Greek Chorus change the scene

Act I, Scene 5

SCENE 5

Icarus and Charon. (A River)

Music 5a. *At the river, they discover the body of Icarus lying by the water, covered with his wings. Daedalus bends over him*

Eurydice Daedalus ... he's peaceful now.
Daedalus It's all my fault.
Echo No, actually, the heat from the sun melted the wax that was holding the feathers to the sticks, and therefore you can't be held responsible for...
Daedalus The wax... I should have known.
Eurydice We need to prepare him, Daedalus ... for his journey to the Underworld.
Daedalus Yes. Has anyone got a gold coin?

Everyone looks in their pockets, but no-one finds anything. Narcissus spots his reflection in the river for the first time

Narcissus Excuse me, have you got a gold coin?
Everyone (*variously*) I haven't / I don't think I brought my purse / No, sorry... (*Etc. ad lib*)

Everyone slowly looks at Midas, who is holding his purse of coins in his hand. He scowls

Midas What do you want it for, anyway?
Echo To put in Icarus' mouth, to pay the ferryman to take him down the River Styx to the Underworld, the final resting place of all souls on Earth. (**Music 5b**)

Midas gives a gold coin to Daedalus who places it in Icarus' mouth. Icarus points down the river to an approaching boat—the Greek Chorus

Midas Who's that?
Echo That's Charon, the ferryman.

Icarus stands, hands over the coin and gets into the boat. They 'sail' off

The Crowd follows the boat and exits, comforting Daedalus

No. 6 Pride Will Do That To Ya

Greek Chorus Everybody knows
How the story goes.
Now there ain't no turning back.
If he'd only known the fact that
Pride will do that to ya.
Pride will do that to ya.

SCENE 6

Pandora et al. (The Same River)

Pandora has been hiding and as they all exit, she appears

Pandora This is so stupid. I'm running around and I don't know where I'm going. I can't trust Zeus, *(to the Box)* and I can't trust you either, so I wish you'd stop talking to me all the time. Now I'm talking to myself. At least I know I can trust myself, and that's good. I should give myself some good advice, but I don't know what's going on. And that's bad.

Narcissus runs on. He's chasing his reflection in the river and doesn't really look at her

Narcissus Hey, you, in the river ... hello? *(He bumps into Pandora)* Oh, sorry. Have you seen a ... umm ... girl with a Box?

Pandora hides the Box behind her back

Pandora *(after a beat)* No?
Narcissus OK, thanks. *(To his reflection)* Hey! Wait for me!

Narcissus runs off, chasing his reflection

Echo runs on and doesn't see Pandora at all

Echo Narcissus! Wait for me!

Echo runs off after Narcissus

Eurydice and Orpheus enter

Pandora sees them coming and hides

Act I, Scene 6

Eurydice Orpheus, do I feel hot to you?

Orpheus feels her head

Orpheus Yeah. Nope. Kinda.
Eurydice Are my eyes red? Does my throat look swollen?
Orpheus Yes. No. Sorta.
Eurydice My left foot really hurts. And I think... I'm going to be sick! (*She throws up into the river*)
Orpheus Eurydice!
Eurydice Something's wrong. My physical vibrations are definitely not in harmony with the universe.
Orpheus Should I get a doctor-type dude? Do you need to, like, sit down? Maybe you should walk it off, man?
Eurydice I need to focus on a physical journey to align myself with nature ... and we need to find Pandora. Come on.

Eurydice and Orpheus exit

Midas and Dionysus enter

Dionysus Midas, remind me why you want gold, again?
Midas Dionysus, you can make things out of it!
Dionysus You've already got lots of things.
Midas Yes, but gold things are more...
Dionysus Heavy?
Midas Yes, and more...
Dionysus Shiny?
Midas Yes, and more...
Dionysus Gold?
Midas That's it! Now come on! We've got to find the girl!
Dionysus I still don't get it...

Midas and Dionysus exit

Pandora emerges. She puts the Box down and starts to walk away ... but is drawn back to it as it speaks to her

No. 7 Moving On

Greek Chorus (The Box) Set me free...
　　　　　Set me free...
　　　　　Set me free...

Pandora Set you free?
What about me?

> I'm the one they want. It's me they want to find.
> And I'm the one who had to leave everything behind.
> It's not my fault. I played it by the book.
> All I did was take one little look.
>
> I didn't know that there are things you're not supposed to do
> And no-one told me how to be afraid.
> Everything was perfect until I opened you.
> It isn't right. It isn't fair.
> Things will never be the same.
> And you're the one to blame...

Greek Chorus Set me free
Set me free
Set me free

Pandora Set you free?
What about me?

> You're the one they want. There's no-one chasing me
> But I'm the only one who will never set you free.
> I can't go back. I have to make it right.
> I have to hide you somewhere out of sight
>
> Now I think I understand.
> Zeus is not the only one with clay in his hand...

Greek Chorus Please set me free
Please set me free
Please set me free

Pandora exits with the Box. **Music 7a**

Scene 7

Zeus and Eros. (Mount Olympus)

Back on Mount Olympus. The scene change is effected by the Greek Chorus

Eros You put what in the Box?

Act I, Scene 7

Zeus Just a few little evils! You know ... mild annoyance ... the common cold ... road rage...

Eros Oh, great. Not only do you ruin the wedding of the millennium, you do it by releasing evil into the world! What's that gonna do to my business, eh?

Zeus Look, it's easy to fix. Pandora has to get back to the house, get married, and have her memory wiped clean. The evils have to go back in the Box and I have to have the Box back. Do you see? The mortals will never find out about it, and everything will be OK. So you just go and sort all that out...

Eros Me? Oh, no.

Zeus What do you mean, no?

Eros I'm not speaking Greek, 'ere. No means no. You ... you caused all this mess and you're gonna have to sort it out.

Zeus Why do I have to do all the boring work?!

Eros Zeus, this isn't just a teeny bit of thunder, 'ere. This is big.

Zeus I know...

Eros No, this is really big.

Zeus I know it's big.

Eros No, this is huge. I mean, on a scale of one to ten, this is five hundred and eighty-four.

Zeus Wow. That's...

Eros Big.

Zeus Look, there must be someone else who can fix everything. I mean, we've got plenty of gods. What about Ares?

Eros He's in Troy.

Zeus Aphrodite, then?

Eros Troy.

Zeus There's something going on with those two...

Eros Anyway, war doesn't even begin to cover it. This is the biggest thing to happen to the universe since the Creation.

Zeus Ah! The Titans!

Eros You buried them.

Zeus I could dig them up!

Eros Not a chance. Look, only the king could make this kind of mess, and only the king can clear it up.

No. 8 You're The Only One Who's King!

> You're the god of gods and you know that it's true.
> In the universe, all the roads lead to you.
> It's time to accept that you're wearing the crown
> And you can't just put responsibility down!

It's the big time now and here's the thing,
You're the only one who's king!

Zeus (*speaking*) Eros, this is no time for a song...

Eros   If you need some love, I'm the god for the job.
With a single shot, how your heart's gonna throb!
Someone to curse? Then Apollo's your man.
He can send out a plague like no Olympian can.
But it's the big time now and here's the thing,
You're the only one who's king!

Now when it comes to waging war, Athena is your girl
And Atlas spends his time just holding up your world!
Artemis will hunt your game

Zeus   But what I'm facing now is not the same!
Eros (*speaking*) That's right!
        If you need the sea, give Poseidon a shout.
Zeus   He can raise a storm, pour some rain on a drought.
Eros   Everyone helps just as much as they can
Zeus   And you've been helping me out since time began.
Eros   But it's the big time now and here's the thing,
You're the only one who's king!
Zeus   It's the part I play, so I gotta sing!
I'm the only one who's king!
Zeus ⎫ (*together*)   Yes, I'm the only one who's king!
Eros ⎭   Yes, you're the only one who's king!
        Only one who's king!
Zeus (*speaking*) One more time!

No. 8a Encore #1—You're The Only One Who's King!

        If you need a sword, give Hephaestus a bell.
Eros   His volcano burns like a fire from hell!
Zeus   Hestia's there, lookin' after your home.
Eros   And she'll be calling you back, wherever you roam!
But it's the big time now and here's the thing...
Zeus   I'm the only one who's king!
Zeus ⎫ (*together*)   Yes, I'm the only one who's king!
Eros ⎭   Yes, you're the only one who's king!
        Only one who's king!
Zeus (*speaking*) A-one more time!

Act I, Scene 7

No. 8b Encore #2—You're The Only One Who's King!

		If you wanna dance, give the Muses a nod.
Eros		They can sing a song about your favourite god!
Zeus		Demeter's feast keeps your hunger at bay
Eros		And the seasons will help pass the hours away!
		But it's the big time now and here's the thing...
Zeus		I'm the only one who's king!
Zeus	(*together*)	Yes, I'm the only one who's king!
Eros		Yes, you're the only one who's king!
		Only one who's king!

Zeus A-one more time! (*He sings*) If you need a...
Eros No, no, no, I think you've got it now.
Zeus Yes. (*He pauses*) So where do I start?
Eros First of all, get down there, find Pandora, and get her back to Epimetheus.
Zeus Right! Married life'll take her mind off everything else.

Hera enters

Hera Zeus!
Zeus See what I mean?
Hera I will not be kept waiting in reception like some demi-god!
Zeus Can't talk now, Hera. Pandora needs me!

Zeus exits with a Flourish. The Flourish will be played by the oboe. If there is no oboe, Zeus can exit with Purpose. If there is no Purpose, Zeus should rethink his motivation

Meanwhile, Hera draws in a breath as if she's trying to inhale the entire sky. Eros tries to hide from her ... but fails

Hera I knew it! He didn't make Pandora for Epimetheus at all! He made her for himself, that scheming, no-good...
Eros Calm down, calm down!
Hera Well, we'll see how much Zeus likes Pandora when I've turned her into ... a snake!

Hera storms off

Eros Hera! Oh, love and marriage! I better go and get Epimetheus! We've got to get to Pandora before Hera does! (**Music 8c**)

Scene 8

Eurydice Dies. (A Part of the River in the Woods)

Eurydice and Orpheus enter, looking for Pandora

Orpheus You all right, Eurydice?
Eurydice Not really. My left elbow's gone numb and my karma's the wrong colour.
Orpheus I don't think we're gonna find Pandora. She could be, like, anywhere by now. Should we look some more? Or, like, go home?
Eurydice I don't think I can go much further. (*She suddenly falls over and dies*)
Orpheus Eurydice? Eurydice?! Wake up, Eurydice! Like, wake up...!
(**Music 8d**)

Charon sails down the river in his boat—the Greek Chorus

Orpheus looks up and sees the boat

Oh no. No! No, man, she's not dead! Eurydice, wake up! Please wake up!

Orpheus watches in shock as Charon helps Eurydice into the boat and begins to sail down the river. Music ends

No! Wait! Come back! You can't just, like, take her! You need a gold coin!
Charon (*calling back in a deep voice smothered with reverb*) That's just a myth.

Charon's ferry exits

Orpheus Oh, Zeus, what am I gonna do? Eurydice, tell me what to do!

Another ferry comes down the river—the Greek Chorus

Cab Driver Need a cab, mate?
Orpheus Yes! Follow that boat to the Underworld!
Cab Driver The Underworld? Righto, guv. I know a great shortcut, we'll miss all the traffic...

They sail off

During the next song, the Greek Chorus change the scene

Act I, Scene 9

No. 9 Pestilence Will Do That To Ya

Greek Chorus Everybody knows
How the story goes.
Now there ain't no turning back
If she'd only known the fact that
Pestilence will do that to ya.
Pestilence will do that to ya.

SCENE 9

Hera and Echo. (The Same Part of the River)

Hera enters

Hera Pandora?! Oh, Pandora?! Come on, sweetheart, stop hiding now. There's nothing to be frightened of. (*She pauses*) Just wait till I get my hands on the perfect Pandora.

Echo enters

(*Not seeing Echo*) I'll teach her a lesson she'll never forget!

Echo sees Hera straight away

Echo Hera! You can't do anything to Pandora!
Hera Where did you come from, Echo?
Echo The laws of the universe clearly state that in the hierarchical structure of the Gods, Zeus must ultimately have control over his creations.
Hera So?
Echo So I'm going to tell him you're looking for Pandora!
Hera You can't!
Echo Can, too!
Hera Can't!
Echo Can!

Music 9a. *Hera throws a spell at Echo*

Hera Can't!
Echo Can't! (*Her hand flies to her mouth in surprise*)
Hera I'm a nasty little gossip!
Echo I'm a nasty little gossip!

Hera From now on, I can only repeat what other people say!
Echo What other people say?! (*She bursts into tears. Bless her*)
Hera Right. Where's Pandora...?

Hera exits

Dionysus enters

Echo runs up to him, crying. She tries to explain what's happened, but the wrong words come out of her mouth every time

Dionysus Well, hello there. What's the matter?
Echo What's the matter?!
Dionysus I was asking you that.
Echo I was asking you that!

Midas enters

Midas Dionysus!
Echo Dionysus!

Dionysus looks at both, very confused, and then at his flask of wine

Midas Quit messing around! We've gotta find that girl!
Echo Gotta find that girl!
Dionysus (*to Echo*) Right you are!

Midas exits, followed by Dionysus

Narcissus runs on, chasing his reflection. Echo runs up to him but he's already on his way off

Narcissus Excuse me? I just want to talk...
Echo I just want to talk!

Echo runs off, chasing Narcissus, who is chasing himself. (Bizarre)

Music 9b

Scene 10

Pandora and Epimetheus. (The Same Part of the River)

Pandora enters, looking for somewhere to hide the Box

Epimetheus enters, alone, from the opposite direction

He doesn't see her as she hides behind a tree. During the following, Epimetheus might turn back and forth, and almost catch sight of Pandora as she runs around, hiding from him but trying to stay close enough to hear what he's saying

Epimetheus Pandora, you're as charming as ... the chimpanzee! (*He sighs*) This is pointless. I'll never see Pandora again ... except in my dreams.
Pandora Who's he talking to? (*She moves a little closer to him, still clutching the Box*)
Epimetheus It's all my fault. I said all the wrong things to her at the wedding. If I'd just told her how beautiful she is...
Pandora I can't hear what he's saying. (*She moves a little closer*)
Epimetheus Oh Pandora, you're so beautiful.
Pandora Is he talking to me?
Epimetheus Your face is like the face of Aphrodite... (*He sighs*) I'm glad she's not here, I'm no good at this love thing. I wish I could be Eros!
Pandora Eros told me all about love. I think he said it makes you feel sick.
Epimetheus I feel sick.
Pandora Oh!
Epimetheus I'm a god! Why can't I just find her?! I can conjure her up in my imagination as easily as ... making the deer!

No. 10 Wildest Dreams

In my dreams, I wave my hand and she appears from behind a tree ... a little unsure ... and so beautiful... (*He waves his hand*)

Pandora appears from behind a tree. He doesn't see her at first. She puts the Box down, her eyes never once leaving Epimetheus

> In my dreams, there's magic in the air.
> In my dreams, I look and she is there.

He turns and sees her standing there, but thinks he's imagining her

> I'm making all the animals just to make her smile

And in my wildest dreams she really loves me...
At least, for a while.
Pandora Hello, Epimetheus.
Epimetheus Pandora, you are... more beautiful than any animal I could ever create.
Pandora How do you create an animal?

Epimetheus slowly takes a flower from Pandora's hair. He takes her hands in his, holding the flower out of view of the audience, between her hands

Epimetheus Close your eyes and wish for a dream.
Pandora (*eyes closed*) I wish for a dream.

Epimetheus opens her hands. Nestling in her open palms, instead of the flower, is a fluttering butterfly

Oh! It's beautiful!

As Epimetheus sings, their surroundings evolve into animals (Greek Chorus). The stone changes into a turtle, the leaves into birds, the vine into a snake; the shadow into a panther; the grey clouds into elephants; the river into a crocodile; the white clouds into sheep; the flowers into butterflies

Epimetheus A tumbled stone, round and shiny,
Glistening in the river.
With a little magic dust
Look what it can be.
The eager leaves of citrus trees
Fluttering and flapping,
Taking off and swooping in the wind
Flying free!

A tangled vine, green and twisted,
Cautiously unwinding,
Snaking round the giant trunk,
Silent and long.
A creeping shadow, black as night
Stalking through the grasses
Waiting for the moment it can pounce.
Running strong!

Epimetheus
Greek Chorus (Animals) } (*together*) I'll show you all my wildest dreams

Act I, Scene 10

>   All the things that live and breathe
>   And stalk and pounce
>   And swoop and soar
>   And creep and crawl,
>   I'll show you them all
>   In my wildest dreams.

Pandora   The giant clouds, grey and heavy,
                 Suddenly stampeding!
                 Thunder rolling through the sky,
                 Trumpeting their way!

Epimetheus The river thrashing with its tail,
                Opening its mouth now!
                Grabbing hold to try and drag you down
                Through the spray!

Pandora (*speaking*) Epimetheus!

Epimetheus
Greek Chorus (Animals) } (*together*) I'll save you in my wildest dreams
                 From the things that live and breathe
                 And stalk and pounce
                 And thrash and roar
                 And creep and crawl
                 I won't let you fall
                 In my wildest dreams

Pandora   A flock of clouds, white and fluffy,
                 Skipping over mountains.
Epimetheus   Count them till we're fast asleep.
                 What a dream we'll see.
Pandora   The flowers nodding, rainbow bright
                 Tugging at their tethers
Epimetheus   Shaking off the dew and letting go.
                 Breaking free...

He takes her face gently in his hands and kisses her

Epimetheus }
Pandora   } (*together*) Dancing round and round
                 Soaring from the ground
                 Surrounded by our...

Epimetheus
Pandora
Greek Chorus (Animals) *(together)* Gliding, diving,
    Swooping, soaring,
    Stalking, pouncing,
    Thrashing, roaring,
    Creeping, crawling,
    Leaping, flying,
    Thundering, trumpeting
    Wildest dreams! Wildest dreams! Wildest dreams!

Epimetheus holds Pandora for a moment. They're lost in a dream. As the Greek Chorus become the voice of the Box, they could drop their "animal" personas, as if removing masks. However this is staged, the animals should disappear ... at least until No. 11a Wildest Dreams—Reprise #1. The dialogue that follows should be delivered at a fast pace, and need not wait for the lyric with the exception of the first line

No. 11 The Box Speaks #2

Greek Chorus (The Box) Please set me free...
Pandora Oh no!
Epimetheus Hang on. That's not in my dream.
Greek Chorus (The Box) Please set me free...
Pandora No! Not now! Oh, Epimetheus, I have to go!
Greek Chorus (The Box) All you have to do is set me free...

Epimetheus finally realizes he's holding the real Pandora

Epimetheus You're real! I didn't imagine you! Oh, Pandora, I...
Pandora I have to go! *(She picks up the Box and starts to move away from him)*
Epimetheus No, don't go! I want to tell you that I love——
Pandora *(going)* I'm sorry!

Pandora runs off

Epimetheus —you.

Eros runs on from the other direction and sees Epimetheus

Eros There you are! I've been looking everywhere for you!
Epimetheus Eros! She was here! She was real! I showed her the animals and we danced and I made her smile and I tried to tell her that I love her...

Act I, Scene 10   35

Eros Listen! Hera's after Pandora because she thinks Zeus made Pandora for himself not you which made her really angry you know how she gets so she's on her way down here so we've got to get to Pandora first before Hera turns her into a snake or something so come on!

Eros runs off after Pandora

Epimetheus Right! (*He starts to run after Eros ... and then stops*) Wait! What do I say when we find her?! Eros?! (**Music 11a**) I've only done this in a dream! I mean, she was real but I wasn't! I mean, I was ... but ... I've already shown her the animals. There's nothing else left. (*He pauses*) Maybe I could...
                Maybe I could be her...
                Gliding, diving,
                Swooping, soaring,
                Stalking, pouncing,
                Thrashing, roaring,
                Creeping, crawling,
                Leaping, flying,
                Thundering, trumpeting
                Wildest dreams! Wildest dreams! Wildest dreams!

Epimetheus runs off after Pandora

(*Speaking*) Pandora! Pandora!

INTERVAL

Music 12 Entr'acte

ACT II

Scene 1

Orpheus in the Underworld. (The Underworld)

Welcome to the Underworld, the realm of Hades and his Daimons (Greek Chorus), and the final resting place of all souls from Earth. Dressed impeccably, Hades sits behind a huge desk and organizes the day-to-day schedules of torture and eternal sorrow. There's a lot of paperwork involved, and we join him as he's dictating a letter to his Most Efficient Daimon

Hades ...and furthermore, consumption of pomegranate seeds constitutes a breach of the Comestibles Act, Paragraph 5, Section iv, which clearly states that the perpetrator, namely your daughter Persephone, shall remain in the Underworld for the aforementioned length of time per annum. Sincerely, etc. etc. That should do it.
Most Efficient Daimon Thank you, Hades, Sir.

The Most Efficient Daimon exits

An Ambitious Daimon approaches. The phone on the desk rings and Hades picks it up

A group of Helpful Daimons bring Eurydice onto the stage

Hades (*to the Helpful Daimons*) There. (*He indicates the floor in front of his desk*)

They leave her lying there, as if asleep

(*To the Ambitious Daimon*) Wait. (*Into the phone*) Speak. (*Beat*) What do you mean, Cerberus is asleep? All three heads? (*Beat*) I'll tell you what I want you to do. Wake him up! (*Beat*) He's a dog! Throw him a bone! (*He slams down the phone and looks up at the Ambitious Daimon*) Speak.
Ambitious Daimon I've got Sisyphus on line six. He wants to negotiate a smaller rock.
Hades Is he still pushing the big one up the hill?

Act II, Scene 1

Ambitious Daimon Yes, Sir. He's on a mobile.
Hades Tell him to keep pushing ... and then put him on hold. For three years.
Ambitious Daimon Yes, Sir.

The Ambitious Daimon scuttles away. Hades stands up and looks down at Eurydice

Hades No rest for the wicked, eh? Now then, who have we here? Eurydice, if I'm not mistaken.

A few Very Helpful Daimons cackle

Wife of Orpheus the Musician.

The same Very Helpful Daimons cackle

We weren't expecting her, were we?

The same Very Helpful Daimons cackle. Hades pauses for a moment, then turns to them suddenly

Boo!

The Very Helpful Daimons shriek and run away from him. He summons two Archive Daimons, who bring him a huge scroll. He scans the text

She's not due for years. (*He looks at her*) Pestilence, by the looks of it. And Leander arrived here last night, thirty-five years ahead of schedule, soaking wet. What is going on? (*He approaches Eurydice and waves a hand at her*)

She 'wakes up' and looks around, dazed

Eurydice Where am I? Who are you?

Hades is about to speak when Orpheus enters

Orpheus Hades! Stay away from her, man! That's my wife!
Eurydice Orpheus!

Orpheus struggles to push through the crowd of Helpful Daimons to get to Eurydice. One Very Small And Not Terribly Helpful Daimon manages to cling on to his leg. It cackles until he shakes it off, at which point it whimpers

Hades Oh good, the band's here. Play something soothing, would you? I have a headache from hell. (*He laughs*) I kill myself! (*He has a philosophical moment*) I kill a lot of things...
Eurydice Orpheus? Do you realize that nothing down here has an aura except you? What's going on?
Orpheus I dunno, babe. Shall we get out of here?
Eurydice I ... can't...
Hades Orpheus, I don't think you quite understand the concept of the Underworld. You can't come and go as you please.
Eurydice Orpheus, I can't move.
Orpheus What?
Eurydice My legs won't move.
Hades I say something here, don't I? Oh yes. MWAH HA HA! Sorry. It's traditional.
Orpheus Please let her go, man. I really love her.
Hades Ahh ... how touching. (*He yawns*) Look. We weren't expecting her, so if you promise not to come back down here until you're both scheduled to die ... you can have your wife back...
Orpheus ⎫
Eurydice ⎭ (*together*) Cool!
Hades On one condition! Orpheus, you have to lead Eurydice out of the Underworld without looking back at all to see if she's following. Eurydice, you're not allowed to make a sound. If you speak, or if you look back even once, you lose her. Forever.
Orpheus I dunno, man... I don't know if I can, like, take the lead...
Eurydice You can do it, Orpheus. Reach for your inner child and let a rainbow of love wash over you.
Hades Those stairs lead up to Earth. And remember ... no speaking, and no looking back. Maestro?

During this number, as Orpheus leads Eurydice up towards the ground, the Daimons (Greek Chorus) torment Orpheus until he can't bear it

No. 13 How?

Greek Chorus (Daimons) You gotta lead, lead, lead, lead
　　　　　　　　You gotta lead, lead, lead, lead
　　　　　　　　You gotta lead, lead, lead, lead
　　　　　　　　You gotta lead, lead, lead, lead
Orpheus How do you lead when you like to follow?
Greek Chorus (Daimons) How do you lead when you like to follow?
Orpheus How do you lead when you like to follow?
Orpheus
Greek Chorus (Daimons) ⎭ (*together*) Gotta see it through!

Act II, Scene 1   39

Orpheus   Gonna make for the light
               And I'll see my baby tonight!
               Just a few steps ahead.
               Ain't no doubt, we'll make it out.
               Well that's what my baby said!

Greek Chorus (Daimons) You gotta trust, trust, trust, trust
               You gotta trust, trust, trust, trust
               You gotta trust, trust, trust, trust
               You gotta trust, trust, trust, trust

Orpheus   How do you trust when you can't look backward?
Greek Chorus (Daimons) How do you trust when you can't look backward?
Orpheus   How do you trust when you can't look backward?
Orpheus   ⎫ (*together*) Tell me what to do!
Greek Chorus (Daimons) ⎭
Orpheus   I'm not sure this is right.
               Will I lose my baby tonight?
               Gotta make for the ground.
               I could swear that she's not there
               But I just can't turn around!

Greek Chorus (Daimons) You gotta go, go, go, go
               You gotta go, go, go, go
               You gotta go, go, go, go
               You gotta go, go, go, go

Orpheus   How do you go when your knees are shaking?
Greek Chorus (Daimons) How do you go when your knees are shaking?
Orpheus   How do you go when your knees are shaking?
Orpheus   ⎫ (*together*) Now I wish I knew!
Greek Chorus (Daimons) ⎭
Orpheus   All I need is the sight
               Of my sweet baby tonight!
               If her love isn't true...
               I'm solitaire! And I can't bear
               To think what I would do!

Greek Chorus (Daimons) You gotta lead, lead, lead, lead!
Orpheus   But I need, need, need, need!
Greek Chorus (Daimons) You gotta trust, trust, trust, trust!
Orpheus   But I must, must, must, must!
Greek Chorus (Daimons) You gotta go, go, go, go!

Orpheus No, no!
Greek Chorus (Daimons) Lead, lead!
Orpheus Need, need!
Greek Chorus (Daimons) Trust, trust!
Orpheus Must, must!
Greek Chorus (Daimons) Go, go, go, go!
Orpheus No, no, no, no…
Orpheus
Greek Chorus (Daimons) } (*together*) No!

Orpheus turns. Eurydice's right behind him. He sees her for the last time in his life as she's pulled back down by the Daimons

Hades (*wait until applause*) Mwah Ha Ha Ha!

Orpheus cannot return to the Underworld. He exits in despair

During the next song, the Greek Chorus change the scene

No. 14 Doubt Will Do That To Ya

Greek Chorus Everybody knows
How the story goes.
Now there ain't no turning back
If he'd only known the fact that
Doubt will do that to ya.
Doubt will do that to ya.

SCENE 2

Which One's Epimetheus? (The Woods)

Pandora enters, still looking for somewhere to hide the Box

Zeus enters, in disguise as Epimetheus. This role can be played by Epimetheus or by Zeus in disguise as Epimetheus

He spots Pandora and approaches her. She believes she's speaking to Epimetheus

Epimetheus/Zeus Pandora!
Pandora Epimetheus! I'm sorry I ran away but it's this Box. I have to hide it somewhere safe because——

Act II, Scene 2

Epimetheus/Zeus Oh, don't worry about that. (*He takes it from her before she can stop him*) It's just a silly old Box. (*He shakes it*)
Pandora No no, at the wedding things came out of it and there's still something in there...
Epimetheus/Zeus No, no, you just imagined those.
Pandora I ... imagined them?
Epimetheus/Zeus You know, Zeus will be very disappointed if we don't get married. And when he's disappointed, he can be very fierce ... and extremely good-looking.
Pandora (*after a pause*) Did you say "extremely good-looking"?
Epimetheus/Zeus Oh yes. He throws thunderbolts, you know. It's an art form, really, throwing a thunderbolt. Only Zeus can do it right ... you throw from the shoulder, like this, you see... (*He assumes a thunderbolt-throwing position*)

Hera enters and sees them

A thunderbolt effect can be used as Epimetheus demonstrates the throw, to cover Epimetheus' transformation into Zeus—or Hera can simply tear away the disguise to reveal her husband. The next eight lines should be delivered very fast and almost overlap

Hera Zeus!
Zeus Hera!
Pandora Zeus?!
Zeus Pandora!
Hera Pandora!
Pandora Hera?!
Hera ⎱ (*together*) Zeus!
Pandora ⎰

Pandora grabs the Box

Zeus Ladies!
Hera I knew I'd find you together!
Zeus No, no, I was trying to get her to go back to Epimetheus, just listen for once...!
Pandora He was trying to get the Box! At the wedding all these things came out and...!
Hera Enough! Pandora?
Pandora Yes?
Hera I'm going to turn you into a snake.
Pandora A snake?!
Zeus Hera...!

Hera starts to 'charm' Pandora. Zeus tries to grab the Box and get in Hera's line of fire

   The Heroes enter and spot Pandora

Odysseus I've found her!
Perseus I've found her!
Theseus Where?!

The Heroes leap towards her and get in Hera's and Zeus's way. They all end up in a pile on the floor—except for Pandora

   Pandora runs off with the Box

Odysseus I've got her!
Hera You've got me!
Perseus I've got her!
Zeus Perseus, let go of my leg!
Theseus I've got her!
Hera Theseus, will you get off me!
Theseus Sorry.
Zeus She's gone!
Hera I almost had her! You idiots!

Zeus starts to follow Pandora

   Zeus, don't you dare chase after her!

No. 15 Stop!

Zeus Hera, Hera, Hera ... my little roll of thunder...
Hera (*speaking*) Stop!
   You can't fool me with disguise.
   I can see through ev'ry one.   **Perseus** (*speaking*) You go, girl!

   I don't want no more surprise,
   You gonna listen till I'm done.   **Odysseus** (*speaking*) All right!

   Come on home
   That's what it's all about   **Theseus** (*speaking*) Testify!
   Or baby I am moving out!
   So listen up! You better stop!
                                   Heroes Stop, stop, stop, stop, stop!
   Stop your messin' me around!

Act II, Scene 2

Zeus Hera!
Hera Don't you make another sound!

    I'm gonna chase you till you drop
    So listen up! You better stop!

    You were a bull for Europa
    You went bathing on a whim.
    At least you could have found
    A girl who knew how to swim.
    Come on home
    That's what it's all about
    Or baby I am moving out!
    So listen up! You better stop!

    Stop your messin' me around!

    Don't you make another sound!

    I'm gonna chase you till you drop
    So listen up!
    You better stop!

Instrumental Dance Break

    You better stop!

    Stop your messin' me around

    Don't you make another sound!

    I'm gonna chase you till you drop
    So listen up!

    You better stop!
    Stop your messin' me around!
    Don't you make another sound!

    Don't mess around!

Heroes Not one sound!

    You better stop!

    Oo...
    Wah...
    Oo...
    Wah...
    Bop bop bop bop
    Bop bop bop bop
    Oo... wah!
    Stop,
    Stop, stop, stop, stop!

    Don't mess around!

    Not one sound!

    You better stop!
    2, 3, 4, 5, 6, 7!

    Stop,
    Stop, stop, stop, stop!

    Don't mess around!

    Not one sound!

    Stop, stop, stop, stop, stop!
    Stop, stop, stop, stop, stop!
    Stop, stop, stop, stop, stop!

> I'm gonna chase you till you
> drop
> So listen up!
> You better stop! You better stop!

Zeus Why does everyone want to sing at me today?
Hera I think now would be the perfect time for you to apologise, don't you, Zeus?
Zeus But Hera, you've got it all wrong! If I don't get hold of Pandora, it could mean disaster for all the gods! I'm telling you the truth, woman!

The Heroes look at Hera

Hera You just can't say sorry, can you? Fine. I'll deal with her. And you'd better stay out of my way!

Hera stomps off, The Heroes stomp off after her

Zeus (*aside*) Oh, Hades! (*He pauses*) Hades! Evil is his department! Maybe he'll help me get all the evils back! By Me, I'm a genius!

Zeus exits

The Greek Chorus change the scene. **Music 15a**

Scene 3

Echo and Narcissus. (A Flowery Part of the River)

Narcissus runs on, chasing his reflection. He stops and talks to the image in the river

Narcissus Hello? Um, hello. My name's Narcissus. And you are...? (*He reaches his hand out to his reflection as if to shake hands, but as soon as he touches the water, the reflection is spoiled*)

Echo runs on, and up to Narcissus ... on the other side of the river

She speaks and sings to him, and he to his reflection

> Hello?
> **Echo** Hello?
> **Narcissus** It's not fair.

Act II, Scene 3

Echo It's not fair!
Narcissus I love you, but you won't even talk to me.
Echo Talk to me?

No. 16 Say That You Love Me

Narcissus What am I going to do?
Echo What am I going to do?

Narcissus There you are,	**Echo** There you are
Perfect and real.	Perfect and real
The smile on your face	
Says you feel what I feel	Feel what I feel
But ev'ry time I touch you	Oo-oo
You disappear from view.	Oo oo-oo-oo
Oh stay	Stay
And say	Say
That you love me!	Love me
There you are,	There you are
Loving and true	Loving and true
And even the flowers	
Are reaching for you,	Reaching for you
But every time they touch you	Oo-oo oo
You disappear from view.	Oo oo oo
Oh stay	Stay
And say	Say
That you love me!	Love me
Please don't tease me so!	Oh oh oh oh!
Oh, tell me what to do!	Oo oo oo oo!
You won't say yes or no!	Oh oh oh oh!
Baby, I'm so blue!	(*Sobbingly*) A. E. I. O. U!

Little Flower Dance. During the rest of the song, the following transformations are gradually facilitated by the Greek Chorus. As Narcissus sits longingly by the river, he grows roots into the earth and pines himself into a flower. Echo tries in vain to make him hear her words. She pines away until nothing is left of her but her voice

Here I am,	Here I am
Here I will stay.	Here I will stay
I look in your eyes	
And the world fades away,	World fades away
But every time I touch you	Oo oo oo

You disappear from view.	Oo oo oo
Oh stay	Stay
And say	Say
That you love me!	Love me
Oh stay	Stay
And say	Say
That you love me... love me...	Love me... love me...

Greek Chorus (Echo's Voice) Love me, love me, love me,
    Love me, love me, love me...

Their transformations are complete. Narcissus freezes as a flower (Greek Chorus) and Echo's voice (Greek Chorus) is all that's left of her. During the next song, the Greek Chorus change the scene

No. 17 Vanity Will Do That To Ya

Greek Chorus Everybody knows
    How the story goes.
    Now there ain't no turning back.
    If he'd only known the fact that
    Vanity will do that to ya.
    Vanity will do that to ya.

Scene 4

Midas and Dionysus. (In The Woods)

Midas and Dionysus enter. Dionysus is very drunk and rather tired. Midas is frantically looking for the Box

Midas ...and I can't believe no-one else had any money. It's a conspiracy! They're all after my gold! Where is that Box... I mean, girl?
Dionysus (*belching*) Pardon me! I 'spect she's gone somewhere comfy to have a nap...
Midas You're drunk!
Dionysus Which one of you said that?
Midas Ugh. She's hiding round here somewhere. We need to flush her out. Can you make the wind blow really hard?
Dionysus Yep! (*He waves his hands around impressively.* **Music 17a**)

A heavy wind springs up and the two men are blown around. They both shout over the wind

Act II, Scene 4   47

Midas I can't see her, can you?
Dionysus What did you say?
Midas It's not working!
Dionysus What?!
Midas Make the wind stop!
Dionysus I can't hear you over this wind! (*He waves his hands around impressively*)

The wind stops. Midas falls over

Midas (*shouting*) Make the wind...! Darn it, Dionysus! Make it hot! Make it very hot! That'll flush her out of the foliage.
Dionysus Hot. Right you are. (*He makes it very hot.* **Music 17b**)
Midas Come on, Pandora. Bring me the Box. Come out, come out, wherever you are...
Dionysus This'll never work.
Midas It might.
Dionysus She was born in an oven at three thousand degrees. I don't think she minds the heat. Hic!
Midas Oh, well, you think of something then!

Dionysus absentmindedly waves one hand a bit. The heat stops

Dionysus I think I'll have a bit of a nap. (*He sits down on the ground under a tree*)
Midas One more, one more. Make it cold!
Dionysus What?
Midas Make it cold!
Dionysus Argh! It's always gold, gold, gold! You make it gold! (*He waves his hand at Midas.* **Music 17c**)
Midas Dionysus, I said cold, not ... gold!

No. 18 Gold Fever

Midas touches something. It turns to gold, facilitated by the Greek Chorus. He does a double take

> Did I just do that? (*He turns something else to gold*) Gold! Wonder if I can do it again? (*Again he turns something to gold*) Whoa! Why didn't we do this before?!

Everything Midas touches turns to gold. (Well, there's a whole myth in one sentence)

> I have the power!

Don't think of zinc, that ain't my
   lode
And copper will corrode.
Just follow popularity
Nickel is for charity.
Currency, financial gain
Wanna watch me jump the train?
My standard's high   **Greek Chorus** Standard's high
And that's the reason why I got   Reason why
   the...

Gold fever   G-O-L-D fever
(*Speaking*) Do ya dig?
Gold fever   G-O-L-D fever

Don't make my palette primaries
I ain't that hard to please
Don't wanna paint the city red
Didn't you hear what I said?
Sink the pink, take back the black.
Nothing green between us, Jack.
I won't be blue   Won't be blue
So long as I am true to...   I am true

Gold fever   G-O-L-D fever
(*Speaking*) Do ya dig?
Gold fever   G-O-L-D fever
Gold, gold fever!   G-O-L-D G-O-L-D fever

Do the sift   Ooo...
Do the rush   Rushhhhh!
Do the glitter   Ooo...
Do the dust   Dussssst
Do the carat   Twenty-four
Do the shine   Shine!
Do the chain   Chay-yay...
Now ain't it fine? That...   ...yay-yayn

Gold fever   G-O-L-D fever
(*Speaking*) Do ya dig?
Gold fever   G-O-L-D fever

Gold fever   G-O-L-D fever

Act II, Scene 5

(*Speaking*) Do ya dig?
Gold fever
Gold, gold fever!

G-O-L-D fever
G-O-L-D G-O-L-D fever

The Greek Chorus actually turn Midas into gold

Hey! What's going on?! I'm
turning gold! Somebody help me!
Help! Help! Ahh...!
Go-wo-wo-wold fever!

G-O-L-D G-O-L-D
G-O-L-D G-O-L-D

G-O-L-D fever!

During the next song, the Greek Chorus change the scene

No. 19 Greed Will Do That To Ya

Greek Chorus Everybody knows
How the story goes.
Now there ain't no turning back.
If he'd only known the fact that
Greed will do that to ya.
Greed will do that to ya.

SCENE 5

Zeus and Hades. (The Underworld)

Zeus and Hades are in the middle of a conversation. The Greek Chorus can play Daimons in this scene if required

Hades ...and now my schedule, to coin a phrase, has gone all to hell because of your "little joke"! I can't believe you did this. I had a release of evils scheduled three thousand years from now.
Zeus But we'll just get all the evils back and everything will be——
Hades No, no, no. Getting all the evils back just isn't feasible.
Zeus Why not?
Hades Zeus, evil doesn't just stay where you put it. It spreads. It has an incredible distribution system. By now it'll be completely hidden in a million places. It's a management nightmare, it really is.
Zeus So what do I do?!
Hades You know... Brother ... it occurs to me that this is the ideal opportunity for a very rewarding merger.
Zeus Merger?

Hades Yes, yes. If we join forces, so to speak, I could cunningly manipulate the evils you've put on Earth... let's call me Director of Operations... and when the mortals are suffering in complete degradation and despair... (*he pauses*) they could come crawling to you, Zeus... Director of Divine Forgiveness!

Zeus's expression of excitement and enthusiasm takes a moment to turn to confusion

Zeus I'm not with you.
Hades I know. But you should be.

No. 20 The "It-Takes-Two-To-Tango" Tango

You do good in your realm and I do bad in mine
But what if we should let our talents intertwine?
Torturing the dead is amusing for a while
But torturing the living would really make me smile...

Let's do the it-takes-two-to-tango tango.
Come dance with me upon that moonlit shore
Where waves of evil ebb and flow
Upon the sands of good.
We'll sway beneath the waning moon
As all true lovers should.

Let's do the it-takes-two-to-tango tango.
A solo gets to be an awful bore.
But now you have me in your arms
And in my arms there's you.
Just think of the delicious things
The two of us can do!

	It takes two to...
Zeus	Walk down the aisle
Hades	Get a divorce
Zeus	Kiss and make up
Hades	Or break up
Zeus	Of course!
	It takes two to play chess
Hades	It takes two to confess
Zeus	That takes one!
Hades	But with two it's a lot more fun!

Act II, Scene 5

Zeus \
Hades / (*together*) Let's do the it-takes-two-to-tango tango.
Zeus   I'll scratch your back…
Hades   …while you are scratching mine
Zeus (*speaking*) Wait a minute…
Hades   Just think how far the earth can go
             With help from you and me.
Zeus   They'll just be standing still until
             They see point a…
Hades   …and b!
Zeus \
Hades / (*together*) Let's do the it-takes-two-to-tango tango.
Zeus   This partnership will simply be divine!
Hades   I'll schedule ev'ry evil for
             The least convenient day!
Zeus   And I will offer sympathy.
Hades \
Zeus / (*together*) We'll really make 'em pray!

Instrumental dance break

Zeus   It takes two to…
Hades   Two-time your wife
Zeus   There I agree
Hades   Trouble and strife!
Zeus \
Hades / (*together*) A-one, two, three…

Pause, as they both realize they got to three

Hades   It takes two to
             Lose on the dice
Zeus   Or practise a vice
Hades   That takes one!
Zeus   But with two it's a lot more fun!
Zeus \
Hades / (*together*) Let's do the it-takes-two-to-tango tango.
             We'll really show them creativity!
             The seesaw of morality
             Is all we'll ever need!
Hades   I'll rise with love and happiness!
Zeus   And I will soar with greed!
Hades \
Zeus / (*together*) Let's do the it-takes-two-to-tango tango.

Hades   We'll rule the world in perfect harmony!
It takes two to spread the flu!
Zeus   It takes me and it takes you!
Hades ⎫
Zeus   ⎬ (*together*) And it takes two to do the
           ⎭
It-takes-two-to-tango
Tango too! (*Speaking*) Ole!

Zeus Extraordinary! I would never have thought of it myself!
Hades My point exactly.
Zeus Hang on a minute. This doesn't solve my problem. The mortals are going to have a miserable, rotten, terrible, horrible time!
Hades (*smiling*) Yes, I know.
Zeus But what if they find out that I gave them evil? They'll never come to me for help, and they might stop worshipping the gods altogether!
Hades Well, all we've got to do is make them think they don't really have it bad at all. (*He pauses*) Easy! Give them... Hope!
Zeus Give them Hope?! Are you mad?!
Hades Only with an insane desire to torture things. Why?
Zeus Only the gods have Hope! Why would I want to give it to the stupid mortals?
Hades I'll go slowly so you can follow me. If they have Hope, they'll believe their hideous suffering ... could ... end.

A pause, while Zeus thinks about this. Realization, and joy, spread over his divine face

Zeus Brilliant!
Hades I know. Right then, off you go! See you on the proverbial battlefield, Director of Divine Forgiveness!
Zeus Yes. Right. Director of Operations!

Zeus exits

Hades Idiot.

Hades exits

Scene change effected by the Greek Chorus. **Music 20a**

Scene 6

Epimetheus and Eros. (Outside the Labyrinth)

The Heroes run on

Theseus Ah-ha! It's the Labyrinth!
Odysseus Mm-hm! It's the Labyrinth!
Perseus Ooo! It's the Labyrinth!
Odysseus The girl might be in there!
Perseus The Box might be in there!
Theseus And ... there might be monsters in there!

The Heroes exit gleefully into the Labyrinth

Pandora enters, still looking for somewhere to hide the Box

Epimetheus and Eros enter

Epimetheus ⎫ (*together*) Pandora!
Eros ⎭
Pandora Zeus! Stay away from me!
Epimetheus Don't you recognize me? I'm Epimetheus!
Pandora No, you're not! You can't fool me with that disguise again!
Epimetheus What?! I'm not Zeus in disguise, please believe me!

Dialogue over this song should not wait for the lyrics

No. 21 The Box Speaks #3

Eros Epimetheus! Tell her you love her!
Epimetheus Pandora, I...
Greek Chorus (The Box) Look for the light!
Pandora No!
Epimetheus What was that?
Greek Chorus (The Box) Look for the light!
Pandora Shut up! Shut up!
Greek Chorus (The Box) Won't you set me free into the light?
Epimetheus The Box!
Eros I told you!

Pandora exits into the Labyrinth

Oi!

Epimetheus Wait! (*To Eros*) There are monsters in there! And she has that Box! I have to save her!
Eros Yes!
Epimetheus I have to tell her I love her!
Eros Yes!
Epimetheus I have to go to the loo!
Eros Yes! (*Beat*) No! Come on!

As Eros pulls Epimetheus into the Labyrinth, Hera runs on and spots them exiting

Hera Epimetheus! Have you seen Pandora? Eros!

Hera runs into the Labyrinth

Scene 7

Monsters! (Inside the Labyrinth)

Music 22 The Battle

The Heroes run through the Labyrinth

The Minotaur enters

Theseus It's the Minotaur! Leave this to me! (*He approaches the Minotaur*)

They circle briefly and then it charges him. They fight. Theseus doesn't notice that a thread from his woolly jumper has been pulled loose, and his only protection has been unraveling since he entered the maze

The other Heroes move on

They encounter Medusa next

Perseus It's Medusa! Don't look at her face or you'll turn into stone!

They cover their faces. Perseus stays to fight, reflecting Medusa's image in his shiny shield so he can look at her

Odysseus moves on

The six-headed Scylla is next

Act II, Scene 8

Odysseus Scylla! (*He attacks*)

All the fights are raging onstage, in the semi-darkness of the Labyrinth

We see Hera, who avoids several of the monster fights before she bumps into Eros, who has also avoided the fights. We see them talk to each other as Eros explains everything to her

We also see Pandora wandering around, terrified ... and Epimetheus, looking for her elsewhere in the maze. They bump into each other at the very centre of the Labyrinth. As they meet, the Monsters and Characters fade into the background

Scene 8

Hope. (In the Very Centre of the Labyrinth)

Epimetheus Pandora!   **Pandora** Zeus!

No. 23 Wildest Dreams—Reprise #2

Epimetheus No! No, it's me! Please ... please believe me.
Pandora I don't know what to believe anymore. (*She turns and moves away from Epimetheus*)
Epimetheus In my dreams there's magic in the air...
    In my dreams I look and you are there...

He waits. She walks to him

Pandora	A flock of clouds, white and fluffy,
	Skipping over mountains.
Epimetheus	Count them till we're fast asleep.
	What a dream we'll see.
Pandora ⎫	(*together*) The flowers nodding, rainbow bright,
Epimetheus ⎭	Tugging at their tethers...
	Now I know you're really here with me.

Epimetheus hugs Pandora. The Box comes between them. Again, dialogue over this song should continue regardless of the lyric

No. 24 The Box Speaks #4

Pandora Oh! The Box! At the wedding, I opened it and...

Epimetheus I know. It's OK. Just put it down, really slowly...
Greek Chorus (The Box) Keep the faith!
Pandora Did you hear that?!
Epimetheus Yes! Just put it down, Pandora ... we've got to get out of here...
Greek Chorus (The Box) Keep the faith!
Pandora Wait!
Epimetheus No, no, don't wait!
Greek Chorus (The Box) All you have to do is keep the faith!

Pandora hesitates, unsure of what to do

Pandora It hasn't said anything bad.
Epimetheus What?
Pandora It hasn't said anything bad. If it was something bad, why has it only said good things? (*To the Box*) What are you?
Greek Chorus (The Box) Hope!
Epimetheus Hope?
Pandora What is Hope?
Epimetheus It's something only the gods have. When you have Hope, you think something good might happen, even when everything is bad.
Pandora Like ... when I thought there was another evil in the Box, but I didn't just give up? Is that Hope?
Greek Chorus (The Box) Set me free! Set me free! Set me free! (*Repeat as necessary*)
Epimetheus Pandora, there is no Hope in the world! There's never been any evil, so why would there be Hope?!
Pandora But there's evil now!
Epimetheus I know that, but Zeus wouldn't have put Hope in there. Even Zeus is not that stupid. Hope defies evil!
Pandora Hope defies evil?
Epimetheus Yes!
Pandora Then so can I. (*She reaches for the lid of the Box*)
Epimetheus No...!

No. 25 Some Day...

Pandora opens the Box. Hope emerges

Daedalus	Maybe I will be OK...
Orpheus	Maybe I will be OK...
Icarus	We will meet again some day...
Eurydice	We will meet again some day...
Narcissus	Maybe some day you'll be mine...

Act II, Scene 8   57

Echo Maybe some day you'll be mine...
Dionysus Everything will be fine...
Midas Everything will be fine...
Characters Some day... Some day... Some day... Some day... Some day... Some day... Some day... Some day...

Greek Chorus Maybe I will be OK...
We will meet again some day...
Maybe some day you'll be mine...
Everything will be fine...
Some day... Some day...
Some day... Some day...

Epimetheus Are you all right?
Pandora Yes. Except... (*smiling*) I feel sick.

They go to kiss, but...

Odysseus and Perseus run on

Odysseus } (*together*) I think we lost them!
Perseus }

Theseus comes running on. His woolly jumper has unravelled and is very short indeed. The loose thread leads offstage

Theseus I don't think we did!

Music 25a The Battle—Reprise

The Monsters enter and surround them

The Heroes keep the monsters at bay

Epimetheus I thought you were heroes?!
Theseus I'm fighting with my bare hands!
Perseus I can't even look at her!
Odysseus Mine's got six heads!
Pandora Isn't there any other way?
Theseus I know!

No. 26 Lullaby

Theseus gathers the Heroes for a quick explanation. The Monsters are closing in. The Heroes turn to them

All Heroes (*to the Monsters*) Shhh...
Theseus   When darkness falls and the moon is bright,
              That's the time to say good-night
All Heroes Close your eyes and drift away
              Let your dreams come out to play
              Sleep, sleep, sleep tight
              Sleep, sleep, sleep tonight
              Sleep, sleep, sleep tight
              Sleep, sleep, sleep tonight
              Sleep, sleep, sleep...

The Monsters fall into a hypnotic state, one by one. Clearly, Scylla is the last to go because she has six heads

Music 26a Exit of Monsters. *The Heroes gesture to the Monsters*

The Monsters exit obediently

Zeus runs into the Labyrinth

Zeus Never fear! The Director of Divine Forgiveness is here to save you from the monsters!
Odysseus The Monsters are slaughtered!
Perseus We've found the girl!
Theseus My jumper is ruined!
Zeus Monsters are already dead. Fine. Now, Pandora, you've got to go back to Epimethe...

Hera and Eros run on

Hera There you are!
Epimetheus Hera! Stay away from Pandora! I love her!

Pandora looks at Epimetheus in loving surprise. They kiss. (Of course they kiss. This is the kissing part)

Eros Yes!

Zeus looks at them both in annoyed surprise

Zeus You're together! How did that happen?
Epimetheus Sometimes, things happen without you, Zeus.
Eros All you need is love!
Hera Pandora, I'm sorry I chased you. Eros explained everything to me. But

Act II, Scene 8

if a certain god hadn't released certain evils into a certain world... (*She gives Zeus a Look*) (*No, not that look. Another one. Yes, that one will do*)

Zeus Yes. About the evils. Look, it was a mistake, and ... and...
Hera And?
Zeus (*mumbling quietly*) I'm sorry.
Hera What?
Zeus (*slightly louder*) I'm sorry.
Everyone Else What?
Zeus Look, I'm sorry, OK? Anyway, it'll be fine because I've brought some Hope for the world...
Pandora We've got Hope.
Zeus OK, who took Hope from Olympus?!
Pandora It was in the Box all along.
Zeus It was? How did that happen? Everything got fixed without me!

Hera clears her throat

Hera. My little raindrop. Will you forgive me for being a nasty, mean old god to you?
Hera Will you promise me you'll never chase another girl, ever again?
Zeus Ever? But I'm immortal!
Hera Ever again.
Zeus (*after a pause*) Not even Nymphs?
Hera Nymphs and Muses included.

Zeus crosses his fingers behind his back

Zeus I promise.
Eros Let's go and find the others and get back to the wedding!
Odysseus Umm ... how are we going to get out of the Labyrinth?
Perseus Theseus, what happened to your jumper?
Theseus I think it got caught on something when I was fighting outside.
Pandora The thread's still attached. We could follow it out of here ... couldn't we?
Everyone Else (*variously*) Yes! Good idea! Hoorah! (*Etc.*)
Zeus Everyone, follow that thread! We have a wedding to attend!

The small group starts following the thread of Theseus' jumper and wind their way out of the Labyrinth and back to Epimetheus' House. The rest of the characters join them along the way, including Hades. By the end of the number, there is a 'Wedding Tableau' and we see Epimetheus and Pandora as the Bride and Groom. The Greek Chorus sing the backing vocals (in parentheses) in the final song

Scene 9

Out of the Labyrinth and Back to the House

No. 27 Keep the Faith!

Full Company Oh keep the faith
Oh keep the faith
All you gotta do is keep the faith!
Whatever life may throw at you
You know you'll make it through
All you gotta do is keep the faith!

Keep moving on (Moving on!)
Keep moving on (Moving on!)
Every single day, keep moving on! (Moving on!)
Whatever life may throw at you (Oo...)
You know you'll make it through (Oo...)
Every single day, keep moving on! (Moving on!)

Look for the light (For the light!)
Look for the light (For the light!)
When the world is dark, look for the light! (For the light!)
Whatever life may throw at you (Oo...)
You know you'll make it through (Oo...)
When the world is dark, look for the light! (For the light!)

Just clap your hands (Clap your hands)
Just clap your hands (Clap your hands)
When you're feeling blue, just clap your hands! (Clap your hands)
Whatever life may throw at you (Oo...)
You know you'll make it through (Oo...)
When you're feeling blue, just clap your hands! (Clap your hands)

Oh keep the faith (Keep the faith!)
Oh keep the faith (Keep the faith!)
All you gotta do is keep the faith! (Keep the faith!)
Whatever life may throw at you (Oo...)
You know you'll make it through (Oo...)
All you gotta do is keep the faith! (Keep the faith!)
All you gotta do is keep the faith! (Keep the faith!)
All you gotta do is keep the...

Act II, Scene 9   61

              Keep the faith! (Keep the faith!)
              Keep the faith! (Keep the faith!)
              Keep the faith! Keep the faith!

Music 27a Calls

No. 28 Keep the Faith

Full Company Oh keep the faith (Keep the faith!)
              Oh keep the faith (Keep the faith!)
              All you gotta do is keep the faith! (Keep the faith!)
              Whatever life may throw at you (Oo...)
              You know you'll make it through (Oo...)
              All you gotta do is keep the faith! (Keep the faith!)
              All you gotta do is keep the faith! (Keep the faith!)
              All you gotta do is keep the...
              Keep the faith! (Keep the faith!)
              Keep the faith! (Keep the faith!)
              Keep the faith! Keep the faith!

Music 28a

                                      CURTAIN

FURNITURE AND PROPERTY LIST

This list includes properties that are essential to the show. Others may be added according to character and staging requirements. For details see Author's Notes.

Optional set dressing: Helios, the God of the Sun, who drives a chariot through the sky drawn by four Horses: Pyrios, Eos, Aethon and Phlegon. He was traditionally represented as a youth with a halo, standing in a chariot, occasionally with a billowing cloak.

PROLOGUE

On stage: MOUNT OLYMPUS SET

Personal: **Zeus:** thunderbolt, Box

ACT I

THE OPENING

On stage: Bare stage

Off stage: Box containing 'evils' (**Hermes**)

Personal: **Pandora:** flower in hair (to match **Epimetheus'** butterfly)
Epimetheus: glasses (worn throughout)
Odysseus: iron sword (worn throughout)
Perseus: shiny bronze shield (carried throughout)

SCENE 1

On stage: INSIDE EPIMETHEUS' HOUSE SET ON EARTH

On stage: Wedding gifts

Off stage: Large hand-mirror (**Narcissus**)
Small hand-mirror (**Echo**)

Furniture and Property List

Flask of wine (**Dionysus**)
Pouch of gold coins (**Midas**)
White feather quill (**Daedalus**)
Small lyre (**Orpheus**)

SCENE 2

On stage: OUTSIDE THE HOUSE SET

SCENE 3

On stage: As before

SCENE 4

On stage: As before

Personal: **Icarus:** wings

SCENE 5

On stage: RIVER SET

Off stage: Boat and oars (according to staging) (**Charon/Greek Chorus**)

Personal: **Midas:** purse of coins

SCENE 6

On stage: As before

Personal: **Pandora:** Box

SCENE 7

On stage: MOUNT OLYMPUS SET

SCENE 8

On stage: RIVER IN THE WOODS SET

Off stage: Boat and oars (according to staging) (**Charon/ Cab Driver/Greek Chorus**)

Scene 9

On stage: As before

Personal: **Dionysus:** flask of wine

Scene 10

On stage: As before

Off stage: Box (**Pandora**)

Personal: **Epimetheus:** fluttering 'butterfly'
Greek Chorus: appropriate accessories for the 'objects to animals' transformation on page 32

ACT II

Scene 1

On stage: UNDERWORLD SET:
Hades' desk. On it: phone, paperwork
Mobile phones
Office paraphernalia

Off stage: Notepad, pen (**Most Efficient Daimon**)
Huge scroll (**Archive Daimons**)

Scene 2

On stage: THE WOODS SET

Off stage: Box (**Pandora**)

Personal: **Zeus:** Epimetheus disguise (according to staging)

Scene 3

On stage: FLOWERY PART OF RIVER SET

Personal: **Narcissus/Greek Chorus:** flower outfit (according to staging)

Furniture and Property List

SCENE 4

On stage: THE WOODS SET

Personal: **Midas/Greek Chorus:** Midas Touch effect (according to staging)

SCENE 5

On stage: UNDERWORLD SET

SCENE 6

On stage: OUTSIDE THE LABYRINTH SET

Off stage: Box (**Pandora**)

SCENE 7

On stage: INSIDE THE LABYRINTH SET

Personal: **Greek Chorus:** Minotaur, Medusa, and Scylla monster signifiers
Theseus: unravelling red woolly jumper matching his previous jumper

SCENE 8

On stage: CENTRE OF THE LABYRINTH SET

Off stage: Box containing Hope (according to staging) (**Pandora**)

Personal: **Theseus:** unravelled red woolly jumper or ball of wool plus shorter jumper

SCENE 9

On stage: As before

LIGHTING PLOT

This generic lighting plot is a general guide only, and should be enhanced according to available resources and artistic requirements.

Property fittings required: nil
Various interior and exterior settings

PROLOGUE

To open:	House lights at full and open stage preset	
Cue 1	Front of House clearance *House lights and preset out; lights up on* **Greek Chorus**	(Page 1)
Cue 2	At end of The Prayer song *Fast cross-fade to general lighting*	(Page 1)
Cue 3	**Zeus** exits *Snap to "working light" state*	(Page 2)

ACT I, The Opening

To open:	Working light state	
Cue 4	At end of No. 1 *Cross-fade to general lighting*	(Page 4)

ACT I, Scene 1

Cue 5	**Pandora**: "What is it?" *Cross-fade to blue-green lighting*	(Page 8)
Cue 6	At end of song No. 2 *Snap to general lighting*	(Page 10)

Lighting Plot

Cue 7	**Zeus** exits *Cross-fade to open-white footlights*	(Page 12)
Cue 8	At end of Song 3 *Cross-fade to general lighting*	(Page 13)

ACT I, SCENE 2

No cues

ACT I, SCENE 3

To open: General lighting

No cues

ACT I, SCENE 4

To open: Overall general lighting

Cue 9	**Daedalus**: "He's a genius. Ready?" *Add bright blue sky, with white clouds if possible*	(Page 18)

ACT I, SCENE 5

To open: Overall general lighting

Cue 10	**Charon** exits with **Icarus** *Cross-fade to open-white footlights*	(Page 21)
Cue 11	At end of No. 6 *Cross-fade to general lighting*	(Page 22)

ACT I, SCENE 6

No cues

ACT I, Scene 7

To open: Overall general lighting

Cue 12   At end of Music 8c   (Page 27)
Cross-fade to forest lighting

ACT I, Scene 8

No cues

ACT I, Scene 9

To open: Overall general lighting

No cues

ACT I, Scene 10

To open: Overall general lighting

Cue 13   **Epimetheus**: "Pandora! Pandora!"   (Page 35)
Black-out; then bring up Interval preset

ACT II, Scene 1

To open: Red footlights

Cue 14   **Orpheus** exits   (Page 40)
Cross-fade to open-white footlights

Cue 15   At end of No. 14   (Page 40)
Cross-fade to forest lighting

ACT II, Scene 2

Cue 16   At end of Music 15a   (Page 44)
Cross-fade to general lighting

Lighting Plot

ACT II, SCENE 3

Cue 17   At end of song No. 16   (Page 46)
Cross-fade to open-white footlights

ACT II, SCENE 4

To open: Forest lighting

Cue 18   **Midas**: "I have the power!"   (Page 47)
Gold disco lighting

Cue 19   At end of song No. 18   (Page 49)
Cross-fade to open-white footlights

Cue 20   At end of No. 19   (Page 49)
Cross-fade to red footlights

ACT II, SCENE 5

No cues

ACT II, SCENE 6

To open: Overall general lighting

Cue 21   As **Hera** exits   (Page 54)
Cross-fade to red/blue general lighting

ACT II, SCENE 7

No cues

ACT II, SCENE 8

To open: Overall general lighting

Cue 22	**Pandora** opens Box *Snap to light in Box, then slowly fade to general lighting*	(Page 56)
Cue 23	**Zeus**: "We have a wedding to attend!" *Cross-fade to bright general lighting*	(Page 59)

ACT II, SCENE 9

To open: Overall general lighting

No cues

EFFECTS PLOT

The Greek Chorus should make all of these sound effects if they can, either vocally or with an instrument or other mechanism. However, the effects can be prerecorded if necessary.

PROLOGUE

Cue 1   **Zeus** throws a thunderbolt   (Page 1)
Brief, loud crash of thunder

Cue 2   **Zeus** magics Box from thin air   (Page 1)
Brief, loud crash of thunder

ACT I

Cue 3   **Echo**: "Wait for me!"   (Page 15)
Bird sounds overhead, until **Daedalus** *and* **Icarus** *exit*

ACT II

Cue 4   **Most Efficient Daimon**: "Thank you, Hades, Sir."   (Page 36)
Hades' desk telephone rings

Cue 5   **Hades** picks up the telephone receiver   (Page 36)
Cut phone ring

Cue 6   As **Epimetheus** transforms into **Zeus**   (Page 41)
A brief, loud crash of thunder

Cue 7   During **No. 17a Dionysus' Spell**   (Page 46)
The sound of strong winds

Cue 8   **Dionysus** gestures for the wind to stop   (Page 47)
Cut strong winds

Cue 9	During **No. 17b Dionysus' Spell** *The sound of sizzling heat*	(Page 47)
Cue 10	**Dionysus** gestures for the heat to stop *Cut sizzling heat*	(Page 47)

THE ORIGINAL GREEK MYTHS

Pandora's Box
Earth was a perfect place, a Garden of Eden, and Zeus gave tasks to two gods: Epimetheus made all the animals and Prometheus made Man, giving him a gift of fire that he stole from Mount Olympus. Zeus was angry with mankind for accepting this gift, so he had his blacksmith create a woman from clay: Pandora, the first woman on Earth. He gave her as a gift to Epimetheus and also gave them a box (or, in some versions, a jar), telling them never to open it. As Zeus had hoped, Pandora was overcome with curiosity and opened the box. The evils that Zeus had placed inside flew around the Earth. The last thing to come out of the box was Hope, which tempered all the evils. Prometheus was punished by being tied to a rock, where an eagle visited him every day and pecked out his liver. At night his liver grew back again, ready for the next day.

Daedalus and Icarus
Daedalus, a brilliant inventor, built the Labyrinth for King Minos. He and his son were the only two who knew the paths of the Labyrinth, so King Minos imprisoned them in a tall tower with no doors and only one window. The two men made wings from bird feathers and wax, and flew out of the window to escape, but Icarus ignored his father's warnings and flew too close to the sun. The wax melted, and he plunged to his death.

Narcissus and Echo
Narcissus was a very beautiful young man. Many fell in love with him, but he wasn't interested in anyone's advances. One day, by a pool, he saw his own reflection and fell in love with it, thinking it was another person. Every time he tried to embrace this beautiful person, the reflection was destroyed. He waited there, trying again and again, and eventually pined away and turned into the flower known as Narcissus (or Daffodil). In some versions of this story, he fell into the water and drowned.

Zeus used Echo, a wood nymph, to keep his wife occupied with gossip while he flirted with other women. Echo would tell Hera outrageous lies, and talked endlessly about Zeus and his flirting. Finally, Hera became so tired of the girl that she cursed her to repeat only the words she heard from others, and never again speak for herself. Echo was in love with Narcissus, but his spurning of her love made her pine away until nothing was left of her but her voice.

Orpheus and Eurydice
Eurydice was the wife of Orpheus, the greatest musician on Earth. When a poisonous snake bit Eurydice, she died and her soul was taken to the Underworld. Orpheus made his way down to the Underworld to ask Hades to give her back. The god of the Underworld was charmed by Orpheus' music, and agreed to allow Eurydice to return to earth ... if Orpheus could lead her out of the Underworld without once looking back at her. Orpheus almost succeeded ... but very near the top he turned to make sure she was following. She was swept back to the Underworld forever.

Midas and Dionysus
King Midas was foolish, but also kind. A satyr, one of Dionysus' companions, got lost and wandered into the King's garden one day. Midas made him welcome and fed him well. Dionysus was grateful for the kindness to his friend, and offered to grant Midas one wish. "I wish that everything I touch should turn to gold", the greedy king said. And sure enough, his wish came true. It began as a joy, but when his food—and then his wife and son—turned to gold, he ran to Dionysus and begged the god to remove this curse. The god told him to wash in a particular river, and then he would no longer have this power.

Theseus
The son of the king of Athens, this hero faced the Minotaur in the Labyrinth (Crete) in his quest to stop the slaughter of fourteen innocent men and women of Athens, who were the staple diet of the creature each year. The daughter of King Minos of Crete fell in love with him, and gave him a ball of thread to use in order to find his way out of the Labyrinth.

Perseus
Medusa had the power to turn anyone to stone—if they looked directly at her face. Polydectes commanded Perseus to bring him the head of Medusa, in order to get him out of the way so he could marry Perseus' mother. He didn't think Perseus would come back alive, but the cunning hero used his shield as a mirror so he could see Medusa in safety. He returned with her head, much to the surprise and annoyance of Polydectes!

Odysseus
The six-headed monster Scylla tried to halt Odysseus on his trip home from the Trojan War.

Greek Chorus
The Greek Chorus traditionally narrated the story in Ancient Greek theatre.

Pandemonium! (A Greek Myth-adventure) 75

Other Greek Myth Characters Referenced in the Script
Theseus' Mum (Aethra)
Poseidon (God of the Seas)
The Furies (The Eumenides, tormentors of the guilty)
The Fates (The Moirae, controllers of destiny)
Helios (God of the Sun)
Ares (God of War)
Aphrodite (Goddess of Love)
The Titans (Ancestors of The Olympian Gods)
Apollo (God of Prophecy, the Arts and Medicine)
Athena (Goddess of Wisdom, War and Justice)
Atlas (Bearer of the Earth and Heavens)
Artemis (Goddess of Hunting)
Hephaestus (God of Fire)
Hestia (Goddess of the Hearth)
The Muses (Goddesses of the Arts and Sciences)
Demeter (Goddess of Fertility)
Persephone (Goddess of the Underworld, wife of Hades, daughter of Demeter)
Cerberus (Three-headed Guard Dog of the Underworld)
Sisyphus (Tortured Soul, destined to push a large boulder up a hill for all eternity)
Leander (Tragic Lover who drowned whilst trying to swim to Hero, the woman he loved)
Europa (Mortal Mistress of Zeus, who disguised himself as a bull to woo her)

MADE AND PRINTED IN GREAT BRITAIN BY
LATIMER TREND & COMPANY LTD PLYMOUTH
MADE IN ENGLAND

www.ingramcontent.com/pod-product-compliance
Ingram Content Group UK Ltd.
Pitfield, Milton Keynes, MK11 3LW, UK
UKHW021843210426
5322IPUK00022B/447